JUST IN
TIME OUT

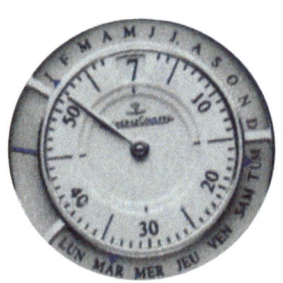

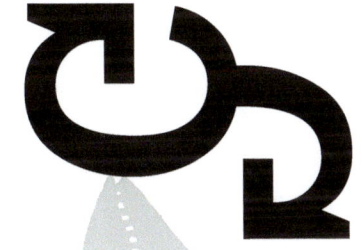

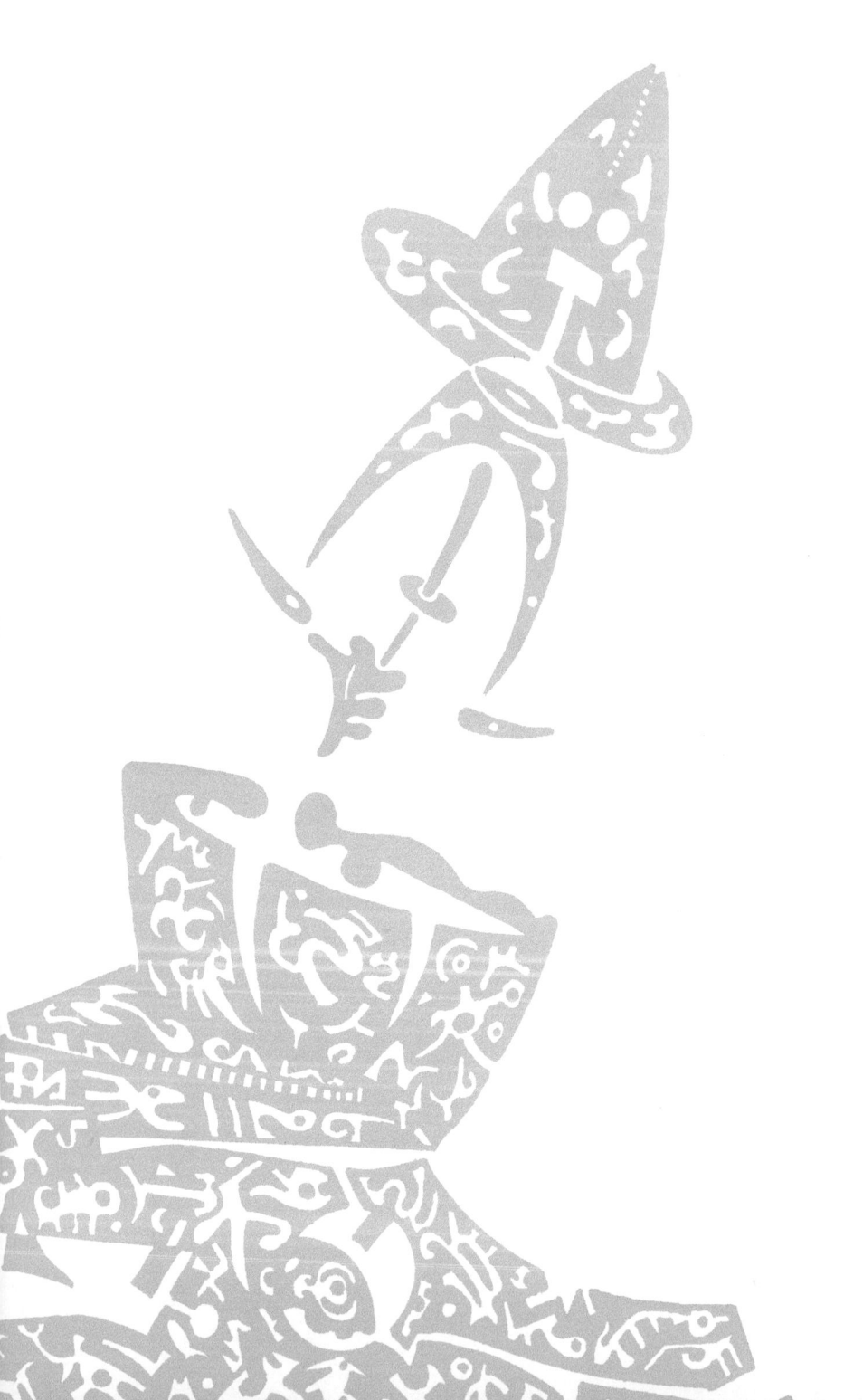

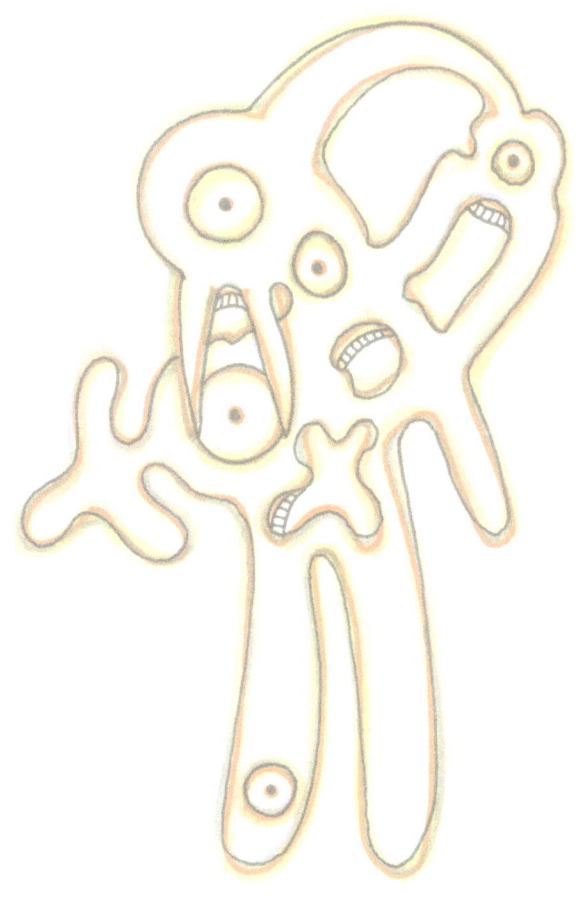

Alphabetap

ISBN 978-1-938521-11-9

Copyright ©2014 by Thomas M. Cassidy & Marilyn R. Rosenberg

LUNA BISONTE PRODS
137 Leland Ave.
Columbus, OH 43214 USA

http://www.lulu.com/spotlight/lunabisonteprods

start then restart here

by **Th**o**mas M**. Cassidy

If Hallmark Hall of Fame produces a heartwarming show about the alphabet, it will be called My Favorite Letter is Blue, which is code for *Holy crap Jessica Tandy and Ernest Borgnine crawled out of their graves to make yet another quirky touching movie about how confused we all get because we none of us speak the same language.* (Especially not the screenwriters! Weepy over how at least beautiful their unsame language sounds, how pleasant a narcotic they concoct!) Tandy is the half-glassed, word-is-good, retired spelling champion and Borgnine is the two-for-one, "happy" houred word-is-bad speech therapist who tells all his patients that silence is golden.

I want to make a t-shirt that reads / promotes / says with a slur

Yield, Alphabet Ahead   or   **The capital of a is A**   or   My other t-shirt is wordless

To Tom: Intro, preface = "start then restart, here" is my favorite.

To MRR: (RE: alphapingalphafluxalpha time)
Page 3 is / will / won't be the title page and whatever title is will be reversed into the red, along perhaps with misc., like store outlets, a warning about strobe lights, a reminder to wash hands. Plus it's a preview for page 37, or a trailer or premonition. Yes, it is into the blank pages that copy need be poured - forward/for-word/far-word copy. I have some on simmer and will finish soon and maybe from there (where lots of our ideas/emails get used) the title will emerge? Has New Collegiate Dictionary ever been used? What about A is for Dictionary? Isn't there a TV show America's Got Title? We might get voted off our own alphabet.

To MRR: Here's current state in state sans statements at the size best suited for not wearing a suit. Have moved pages and pieces a dozen different ways, probably returning to where I began. Have words churning elsewhere and of course title still in Alphaflux.

To Tom: All sounds good! And here we are still in upside down big mess in the house mode.

Alphabetrap   Alphabetap   Alphabetea
Alphabetease   Alphabetop   Alphabetip

To Tom: another again lookseeing - late afternoon's ponderations
wet alphabet

down deep underwater,   web woven mail
below between swimming,   returns time's alphabet
diving, dividing, hiding,   within, wiggling, upturned
   tangled transmutations surface   distant collaborative scheme
   slices, slashes, resorted.   slashed, sliced, restored.

O M G here I go again again again again   agai aga ag a

To Tom: you went first then I added and took away. Here are a bunch of thoughts, variations of same, to be read by you and used in part, edited, combined or not used ast all.

review of early interaction within our
   Alphabet Watchers=time eaters
   space riders become alphabet watchers = time eaters
   interacting, expanding, swimming, hiding, soaring,
   transmutations reacting =
   increased incidence of alphabet's incidents.
        distant collaboration.

OR

Page 64

Chapter 6
If You Speak English Good You Don't Speak It Well: Adjectives and Adverbs

THIEF'S GRAMMAR CATCHES HIM

Polson, Montana (AP) — It's good enough to split an infinitive but if you misspell and mangle you could be betrayed by dangling from your own participle.

One piece of evidence in the case was a note taken from the safe by the burglars. "This note contains papers valuable only for proof. Please fire."

Above the typed statement, the burglar had scribbled: "I read and I leave it He He," plus an afterthought that provided his undoing: "To cops went pass me."

The suspect in the case was asked to write the same sentence and he repeated exactly the misspelled words, confusing adjectives with infinitives and adverbs with verbs.
—From AP dispatch.

Now that you know some grammar, you know that the burglar in the AP dispatch obviously doesn't. He has confused prepositional phrases with infinitives and nouns with prepositions.

Page 60

6. I have (gone, went) home early all this week.
7. He has (ran, run) all the way to tell us the news.
8. The ball is (lieing, lying) where you (threw, throwed) it.
9. Who has (taken, tooken) my pen?
10. He has (swam, swum) across the lake several times.
11. I (beat, bet) him 21 to 14 in the ping-pong finals.
12. He (lead, led) the procession down the street.

FINE POINTS OF THE SUBJUNCTIVE

Although the subjunctive is alive and well and living in France, Spain, Italy, and Germany, it is virtually—with few exceptions—dead in England and America.

Most of us quite naturally say "If I were you," without realizing that what this is, contrary to fact. *If I were you* says *I am not you*. This use is confined largely to *I*. One finds *If he were now* (he *isn't*) perhaps more often than *If he were then* in the writings of modern authors.

Perhaps you have noticed another peculiarity: *were*, in *If I were there* (*I am not there*), is equivalent to the present tense.

Do we have a past tense? Yes, and we use it quite naturally without realizing that we are handling something as formidable as the subjunctive. We say, *If he had been here yesterday* (he *wasn't*), *all the trouble would have been avoided*. What looks like a past perfect tense (*he had been*) is the past subjunctive contrary to fact.

* Not quite dead. In a book published in 1970 by a distinguished British writer, I found this sentence: "Both believed that every work of art, whether it were a house, a garden, or a poem, should be a judicious blend of art and nature."

Page 57

PRESENT	PRESENT PARTICIPLE	PAST	PAST PARTICIPLE*
arise	arising	arose	arisen
beat	beating	beat	BEATEN
become	becoming	became	BECOME
begin	beginning	began	BEGUN
bid (request)	bidding	bade	BIDDEN
bid (make an offer)	bidding	bid	BID
bite	biting	bit	BITTEN
blow	blowing	blew	BLOWN
break	breaking	broke	BROKEN
bring	bringing	BROUGHT	BROUGHT
burst	bursting	BURST	BURST
catch	catching	CAUGHT	CAUGHT
choose	choosing	CHOSE	CHOSEN
come	coming	CAME (not come)	COME
cost	costing	COST	COST
deal	dealing	DEALT	DEALT
dive	diving	DIVED or DOVE	dived or dove
do	doing	DID (not done)	DONE
drag	dragging	DRAGGED	DRAGGED
dream	dreaming	dreamed or dreamt	dreamed or dreamt
drink	drinking	DRANK	DRUNK
drown	drowning	DROWNED	DROWNED
eat	eating	ATE	EATEN
fall	falling	fell	FALLEN
fit	fitting	fitted (not fit)	FITTED
flee	fleeing	FLED	FLED
fly	flying	flew	FLOWN
forbid	forbidding	FORBADE	FORBIDDEN
forsake	forsaking	FORSOOK	FORSAKEN
freeze	freezing	froze	FROZEN

* Used with *has* or *have*, *had*, *will have*, etc. to form the perfect tenses and with *is*, *was*, etc. to form the passive.

Page 65

"To cops" is *not* an infinitive. It is made up of a preposition *to* and a noun *cops* which would make it a prepositional phrase. What is needed is *two*, of course, an adjective to modify the noun *cops*.

"Pass" all by itself may be either a verb or a noun, not an adverb. What is needed here is *past*, a preposition, with the object *me*.

Now that we have disposed of the burglar's grammatical knowledge, try yours on the following sentences concerned chiefly with adjectives and adverbs.

1. Who will be able to claim a deduction for charitable contributions?
   a. He's come to good with the money he inherited.
   b. He's done well with the money he inherited.
2. Which statement has a sick in it?
   a. It's darned good.
   b. It's darned well.
3. Which dog is definitely not a bloodhound?
   a. The dog smells bad.
   b. The dog smells badly.
4. Which one is more to be feared?
   a. He's the kind of fellow who takes life easy.
   b. He's the kind of fellow who takes life easily.
5. Which assures you of an easy climb?
   a. You will find the mountain trail easy.
   b. You will find the mountain trail easily.
6. In which sentence is Joe being sized up?
   a. Joe looked careful.
   b. Joe looked carefully.

PRETEST

1. I can't stand a person who speaks (indistinct, indistinctly).

2. I like a person who dresses (simple, simply), not (flashy, flashily).

    space riders become alphabet watchers = time eaters
     distant collaboration
      interference
   expanding, swimming, hiding, soaring, interacting transmutations,
    exploded, smashed to incidence of alphabet's incidents
     reacting

OR

   space riders become alphabet watchers = time eaters
   by interference
   expanding, swimming, hiding, soaring, interacting transmutations,
   by reacting,
   exploded, smashed to incidence of alphabet's incidents

To MRR: I'm pretty free form when I write or perform so my guidance may not help, but I think tangential alphabet comments/experiences/etc with occasional/episodic mentions of images swapped for refinement, addition, or clarification. Clarify the alphabet! It really might be fun to have a stream of ideas and early alphabet encounters/bouts and general aesthetic approach and tall tales etc. I might pursue three or four "storylines" (mail-art, your work in my Musical Comedy project back when, general anti-alphabet manifesto lines, and stuff I look for when working on top of someone else's work). That's not very helpful, but then again too, this might not be as traditionally helpful as most alphabet books.

To MRR: Churning

To Tom: Subject: luoooooooooooooo
the alphabet twist (sounds like a candy or a dance)
AlphaSentTwist=AST=abbreviation Atlantic Standard Time reference to time and exchange
addaalphabets   aaaaaaaaaaaaaaas
added z to a (do the book backwards)
spellme
alphabet incidents

To MRR: Subject: babalulu
I like the twisting alphabet idea, and here are a few relating to mail/email collaboration.
Blphabet
InterAlphaTwists
AlphAlphAbetAbet
Towards the Just Formation of Letters / Towards the Just Exchange of Letters
Hear Letters Sent
Neuroalphabeticalistic Drifts
No Secret Letters
Melting Serifs

To Tom: listed, I am not sure you have followed by **a** ?
gs you have, -and the **xs** you have, -**lo** you have, -**gr** you have, -**cr** you have it first in the pdf, -you have **he** watch works, -you have the coloring book,- you have the **p**, -the **tjs** you have, and the -**a** you have; I have the following and did I overlook, in the pdf, the following? -**p**, and **pc** yours and ours ? -**f**, yours and ours? -**s**, yours and ours? -tall walls yours and me? -**pe**, yours and ours? -**no** yours and ours? -**mlo**, yours and ours -your alpha bugs and all its variations? you do have one -your alphamoeba? I have a different **z** group -**y**, yours and ours? -your **zn** ? -**ZN** you may have -you do have the **a** and but, do you have the extended changes to them? -you have **l**, and do you have all the variations? -did I overlook the **ehw** group I have?

OR

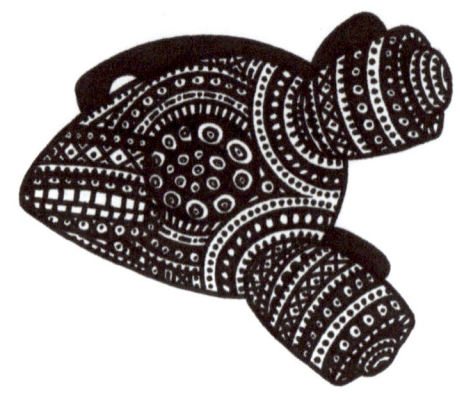

Tom Cassidy

From: MRR [bmrosenberg2@netscape.net]
Sent: Wednesday, September 29, 2010 11:41 AM
To: Tom Cassidy
Subject: Re: STIR THE STONES, TONE SOUP FOR US!

M GO FOR IT AND ADD ALPHABET LETTERS OF OTHER TONGUES AND WRITTIGS!
M

-----Original Message-----
From: Tom Cassidy <tom.cassidy@mmha.com>
To: MRR <bmrosenberg2@netscape.net>
Sent: Wed, Sep 29, 2010 10:19 am
Subject: RE: it is time to make soup!

Hi Marilyn!
This will be great because I am thinking too but certainly not as usefully. I will doodle and scrawl this weekend and send you a packet but all just circling for a core theme – maybe produce in museum shops? poets making everyday situations awkward by reciting lines (e.g. to the bus driver, waiter, cabbie, sales clerk, plumber, etc)? mechanical flowers? An alphabet idea would be great fun to try and push it past all other alphabet books/deconstructions – maybe makeovers that involve surgeries (pop culture) competitions? New This Fall on NBC – America's Got Alphabet.

From: MRR [mailto:bmrosenberg2@netscape.net]
Sent: Tuesday, September 28, 2010 5:34 PM
To: Tom Cassidy
Subject: Re: it is time to make soup!

TOM, SHALL WE START WITH an A, OF aeiouy
or bcdfghjklmnpqrstvwxz
CAPS or lc?
size: how about 5 x7 HORIZONTAL?
now and then, October to October?
The fire has started, the caldron will be found and we will both fill it with fine fixins!
Tell me your wish: I am thinking!
M

-----Original Message-----
From: Tom Cassidy <tom.cassidy@mmha.com>
To: bmrosenberg2@netscape.net
Sent: Tue, Sep 28, 2010 2:18 pm
Subject: It's not yet October and I'm Octoberfested out

Hi Marilyn –
Have yet to complete my inaccurate and boisterous recap of the symposium but I sense the tectonic consonants shifting. Just wanted to initiate semi-regular contact if you're still interested in collaborating on a make-over of the alphabet, a race of the vowels (loser leaves town), a series of back&forth words/drawings, etc. But first we need the focus which, given my fuzzy eyesight and occasional confusion as to what focus really means, I'm game to leave up to you.
Best
Tom Cassidy / Musicmaster

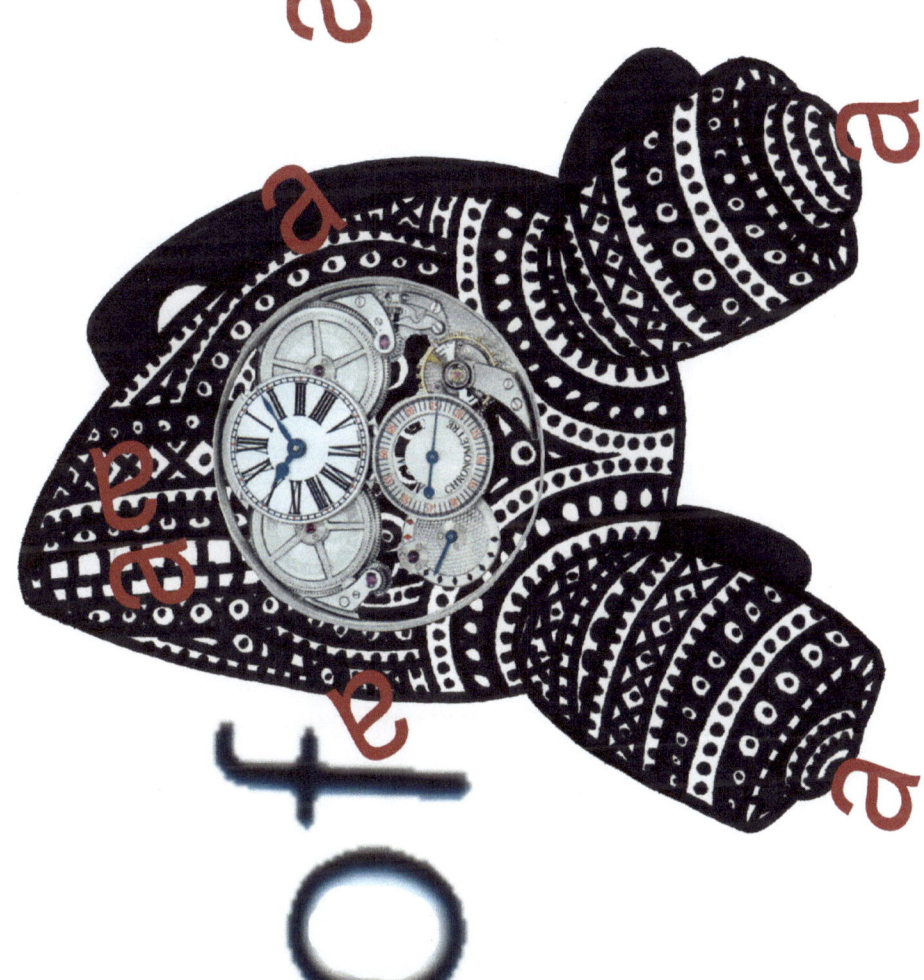

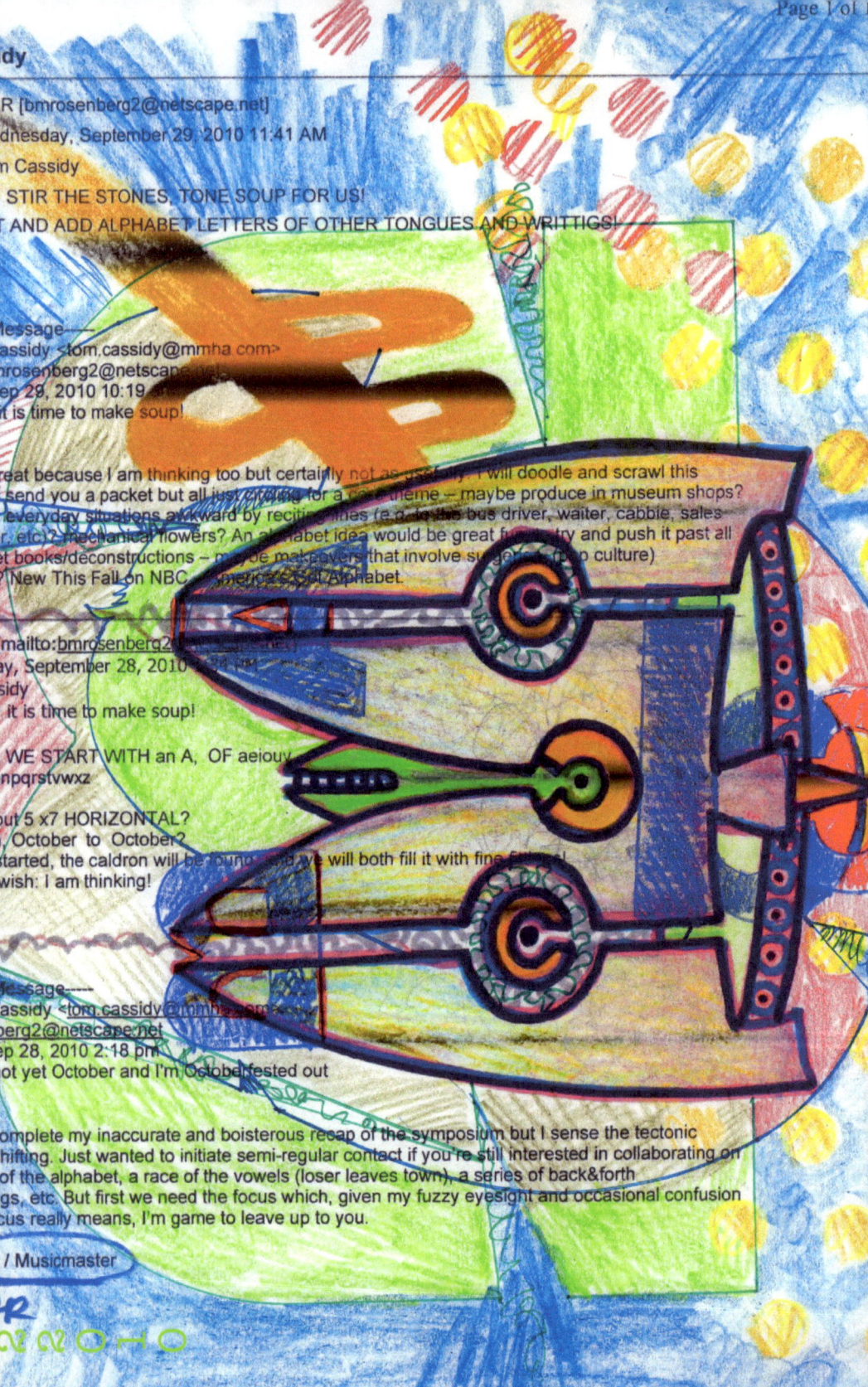

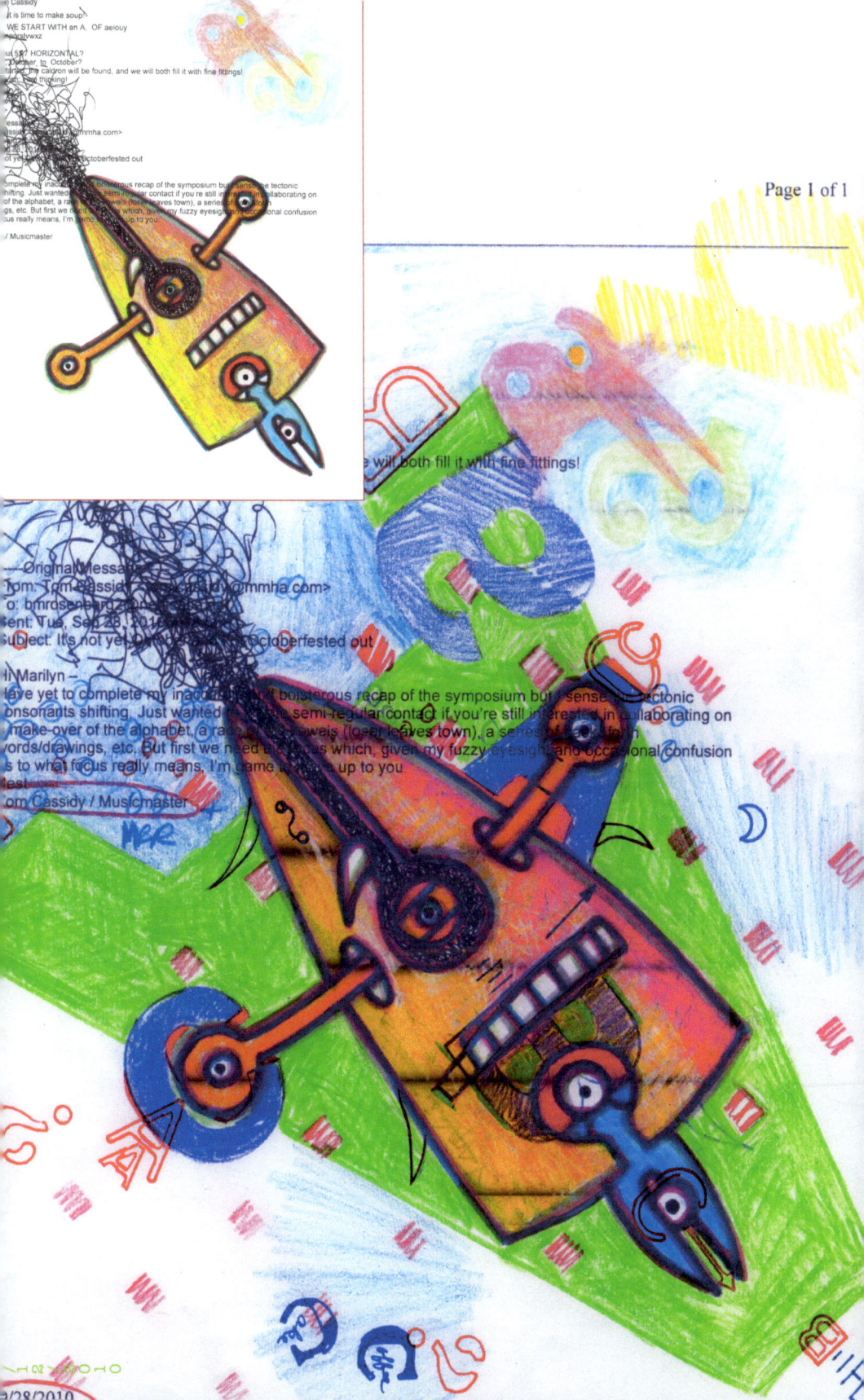

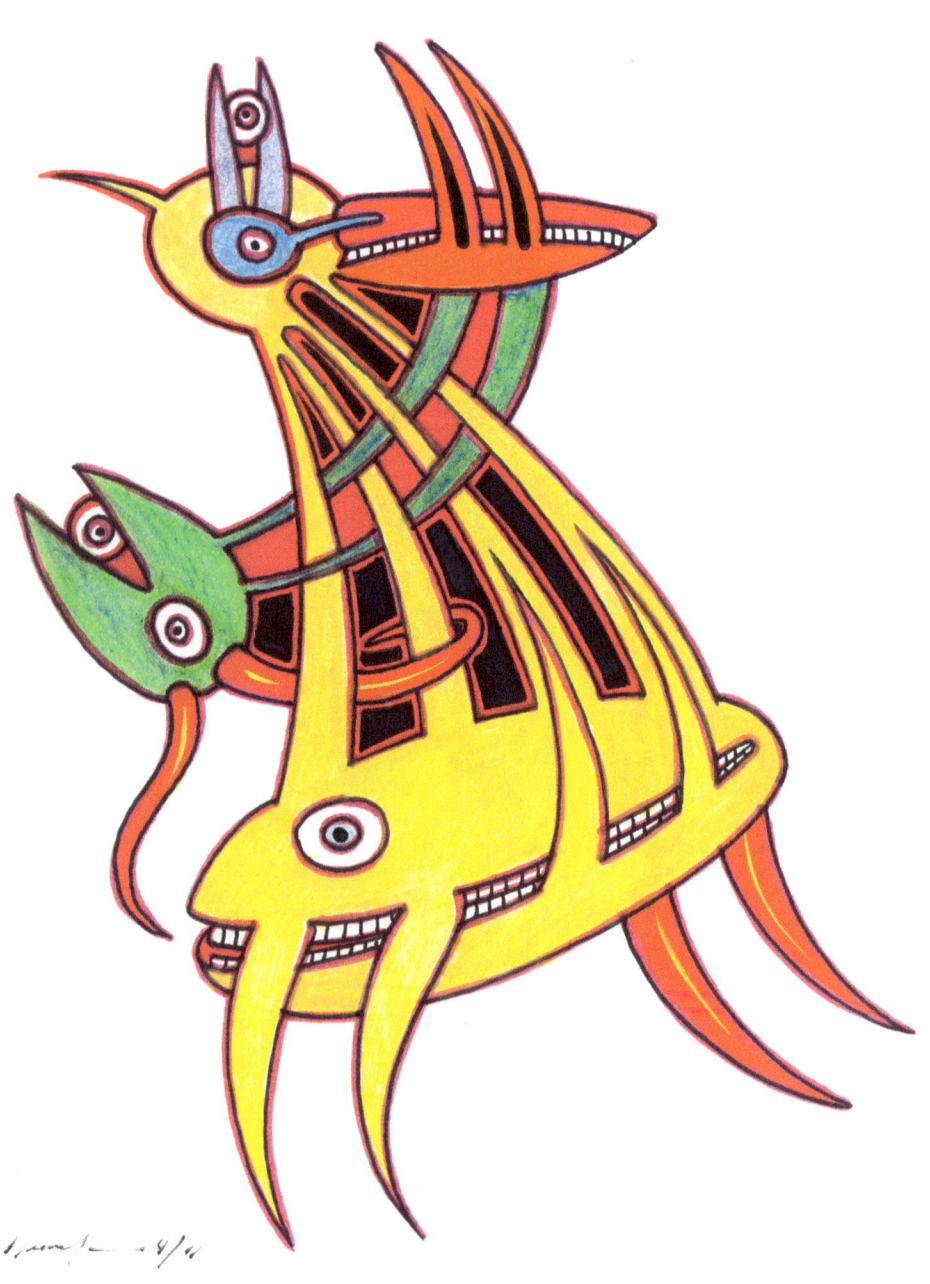

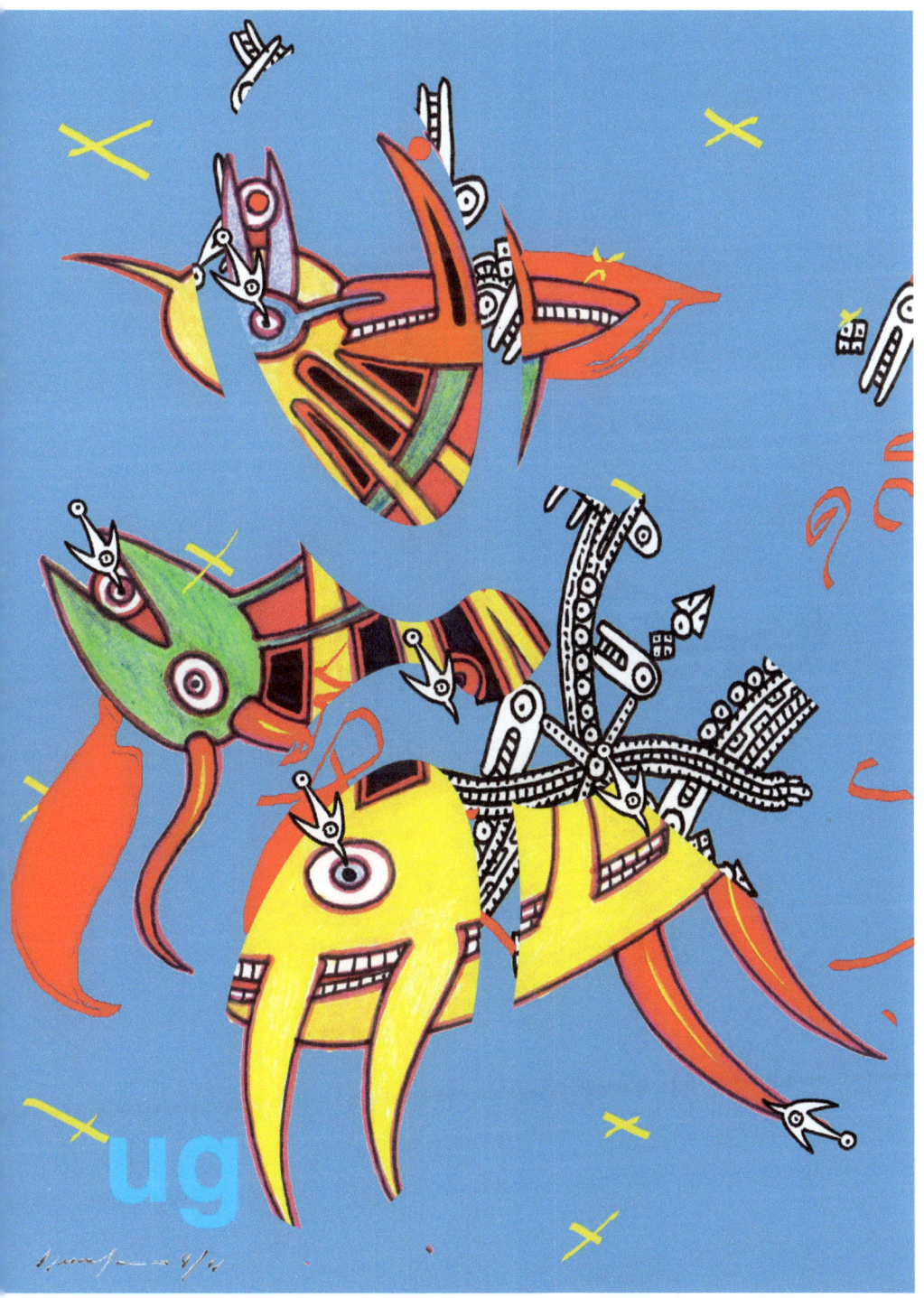

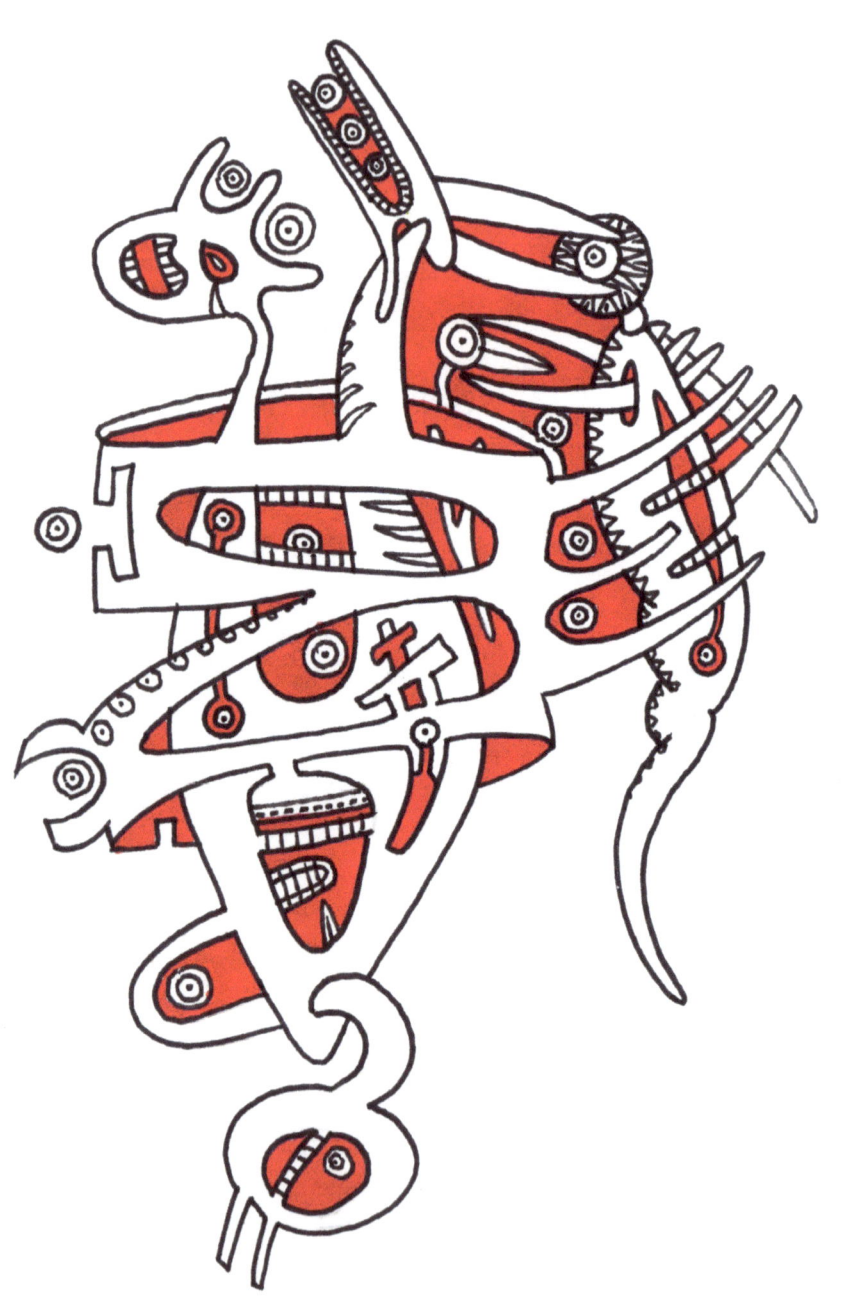

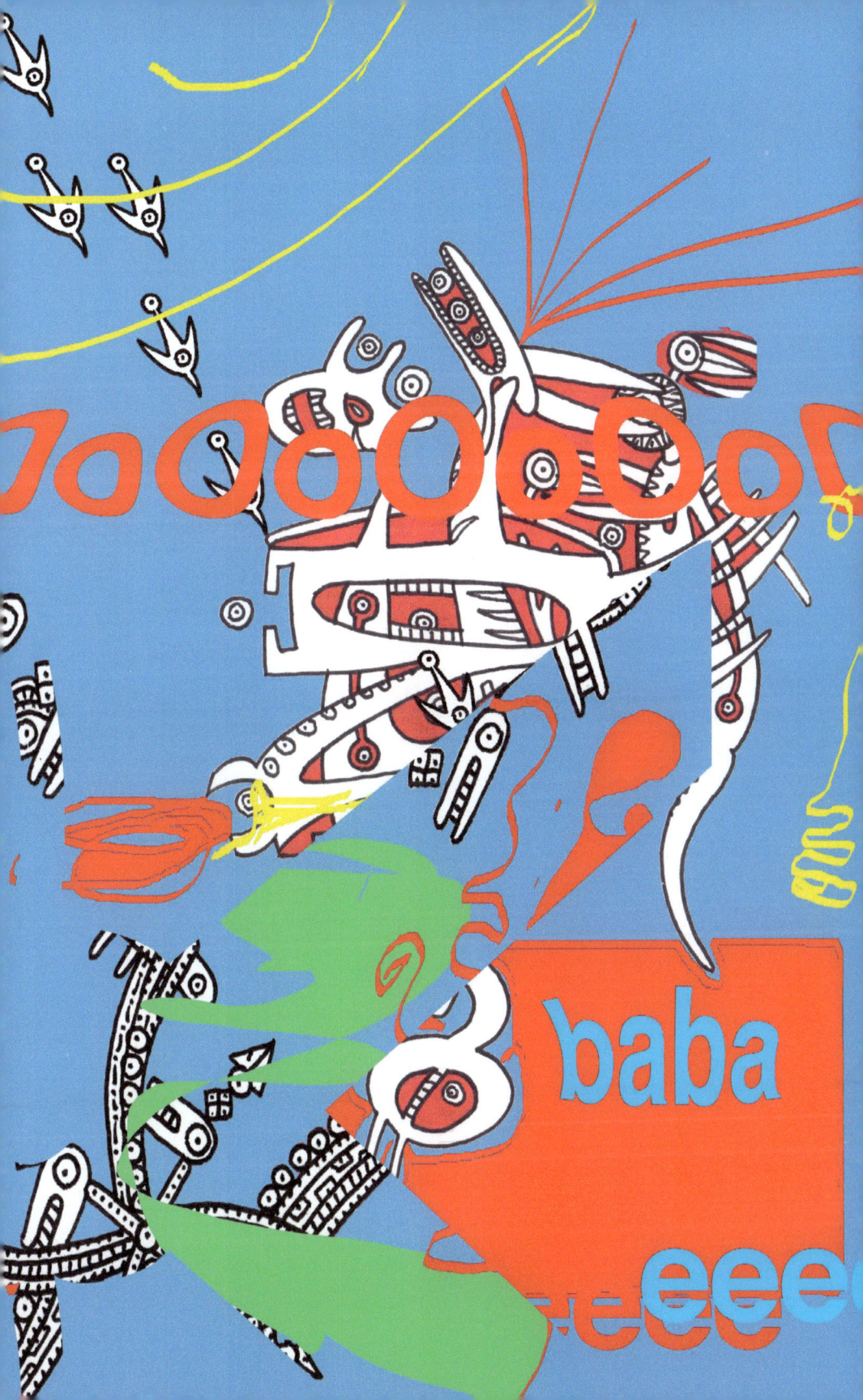

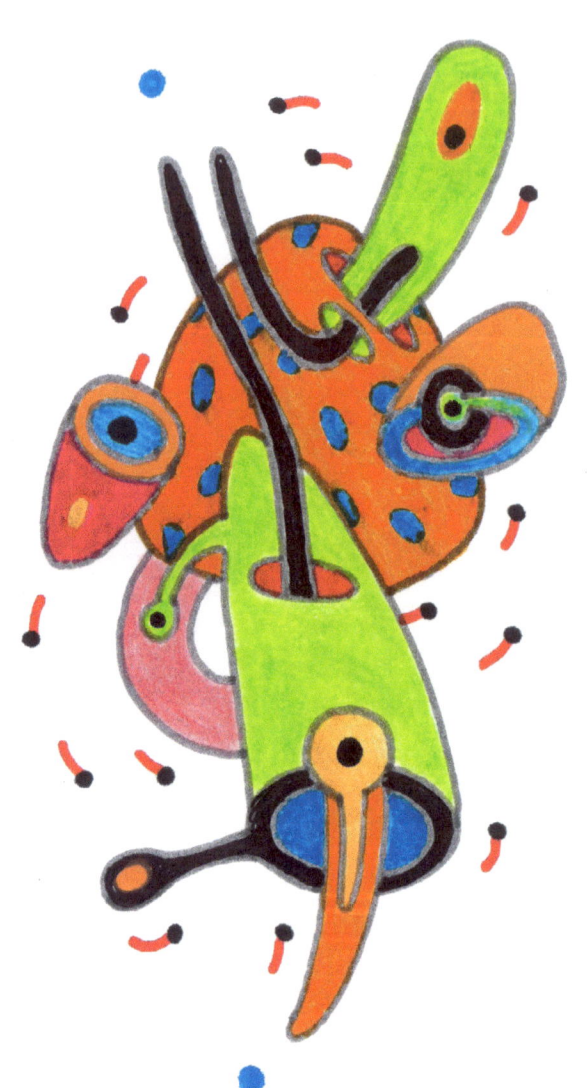

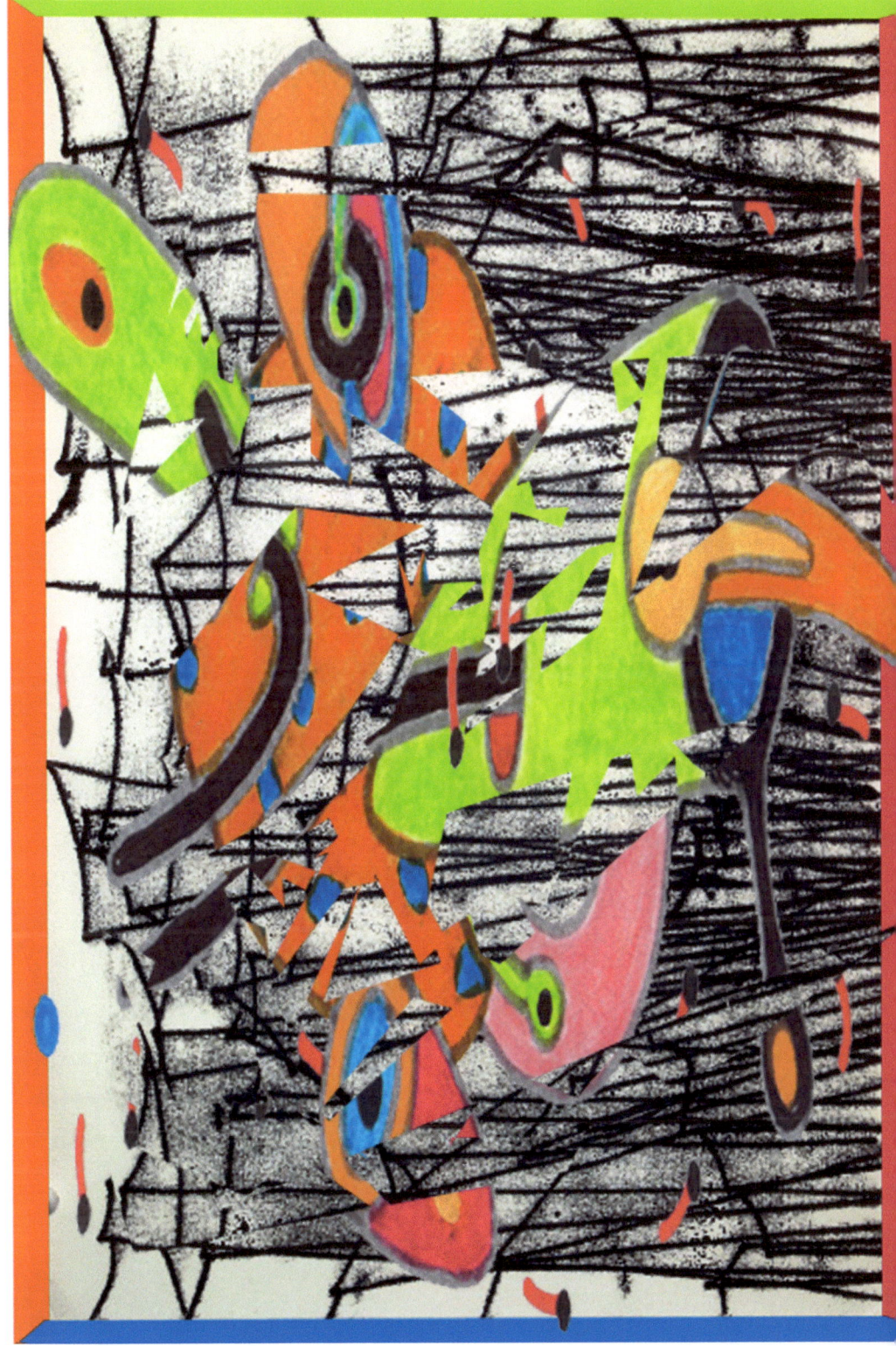

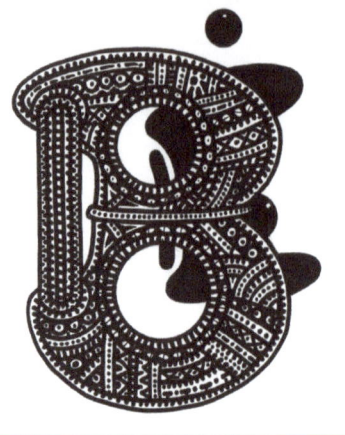

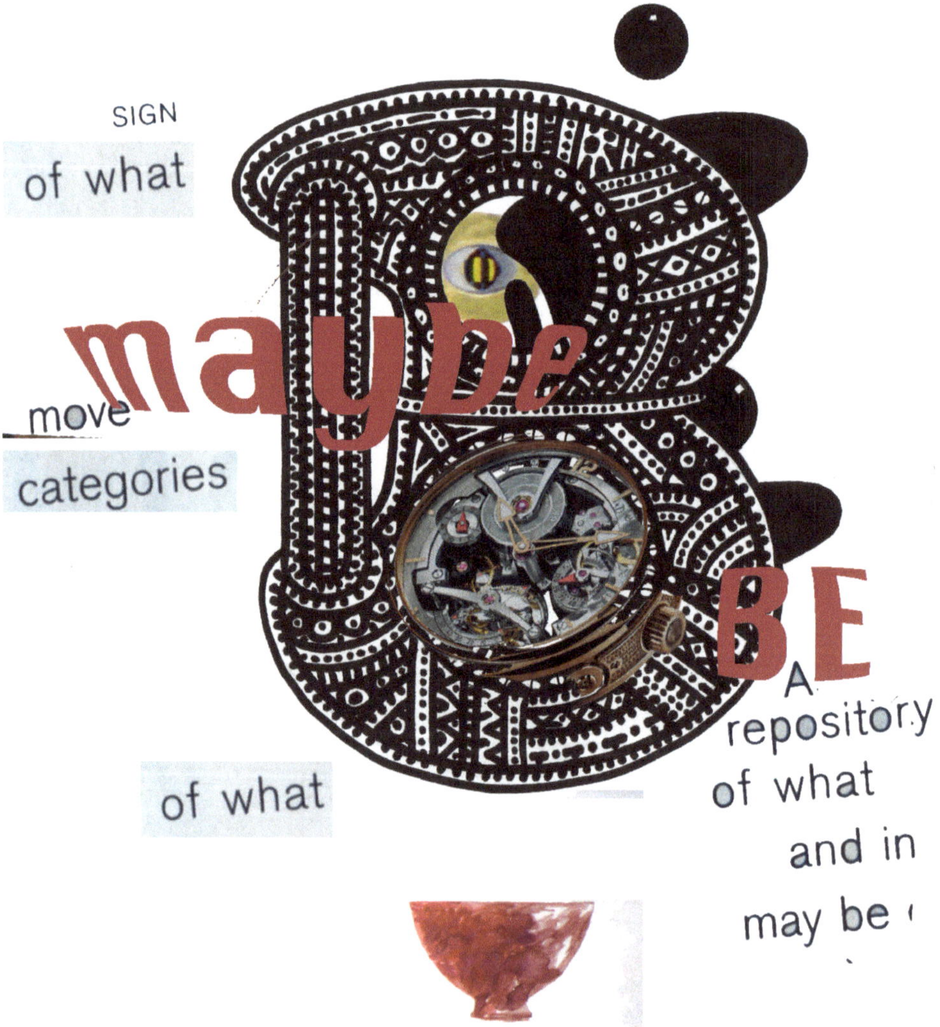

SIGN
of what

maybe

move

categories

BE

A repository
of what
of what
and in
may be

MRR 11/3

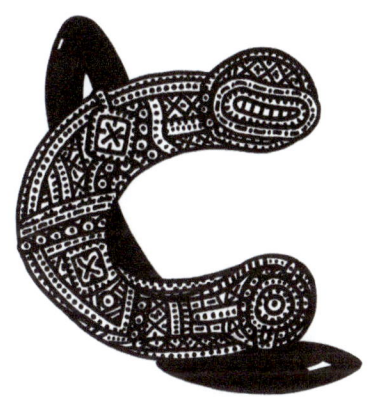

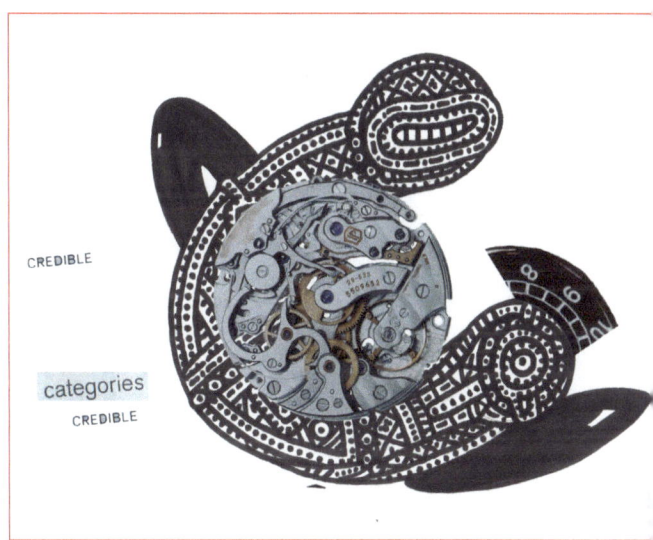

CREDIBLE

categories
CREDIBLE

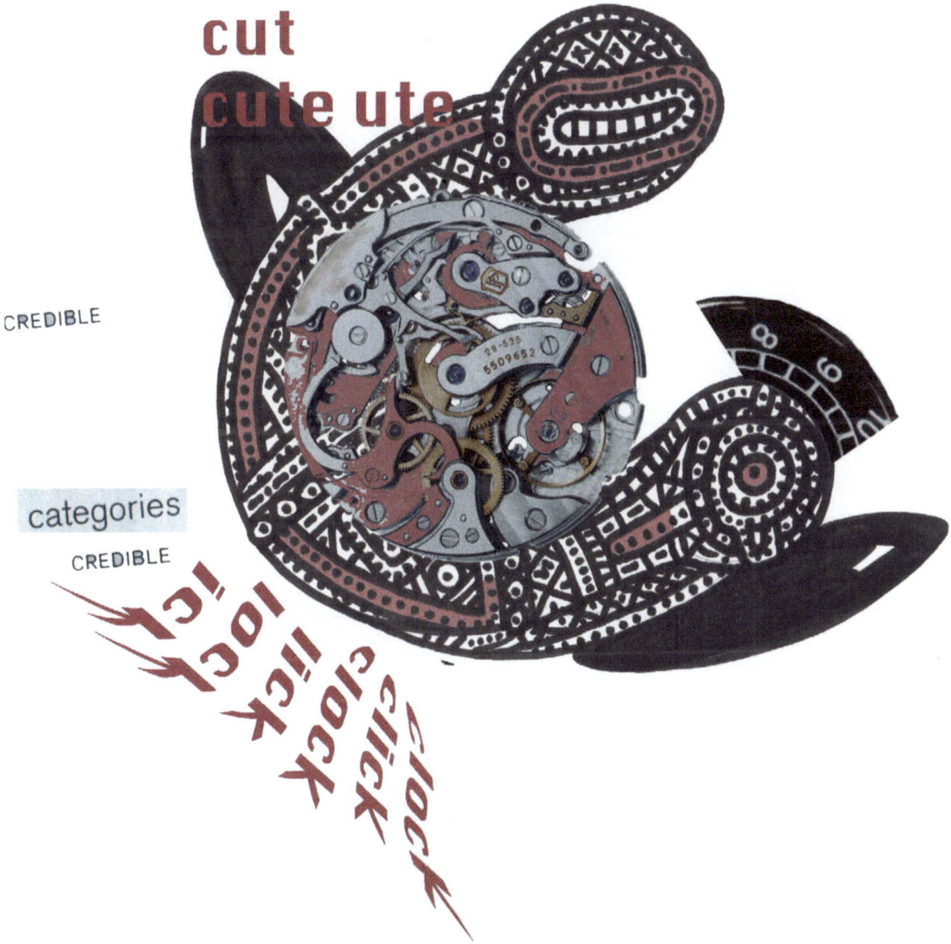

cut
cute ute

CREDIBLE

categories
CREDIBLE

clock click lick ick

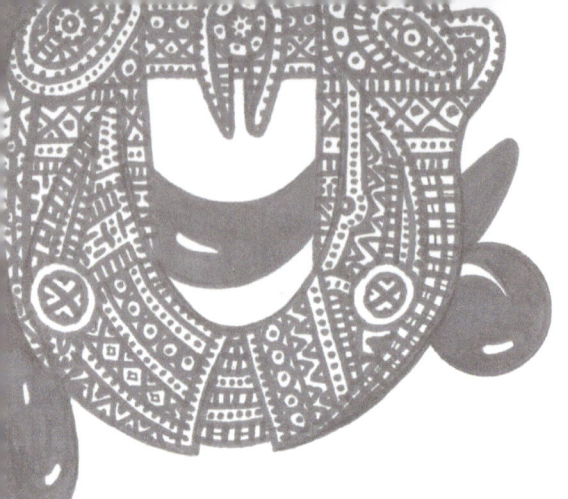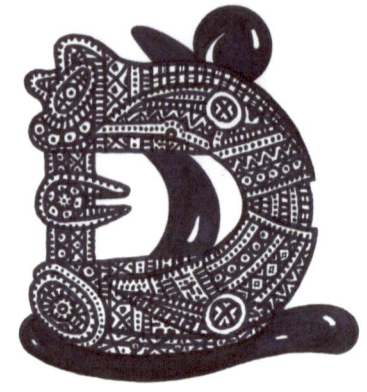

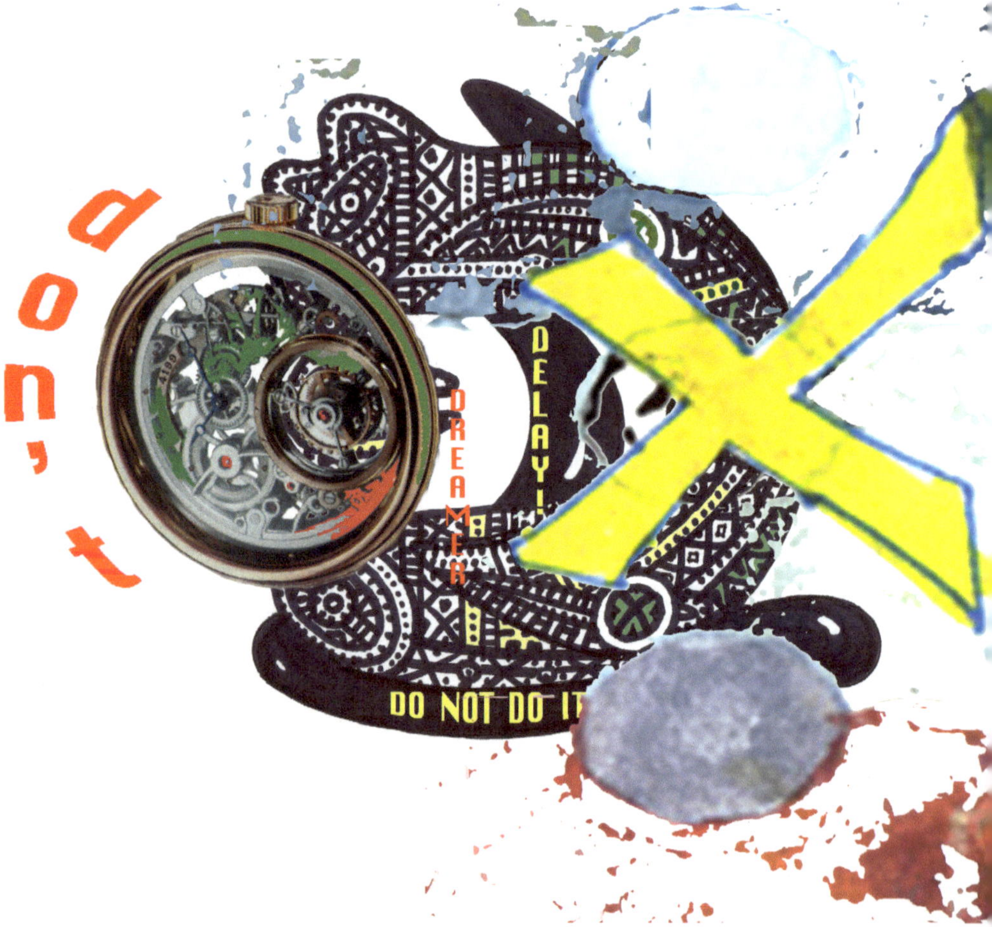

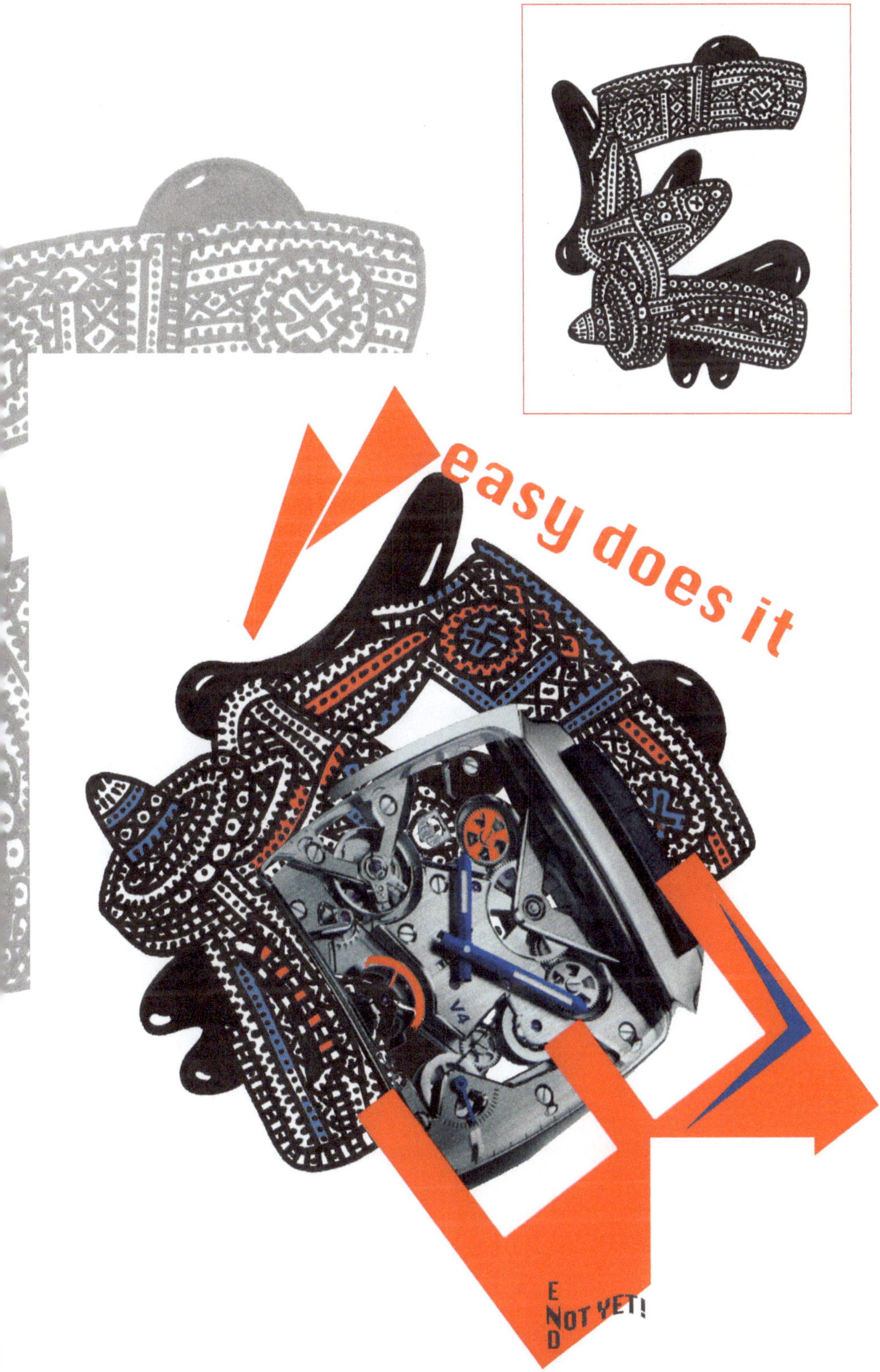

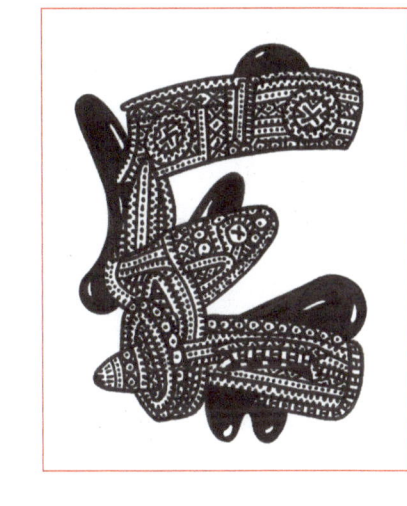

easy does it

E
NOT YET!
D

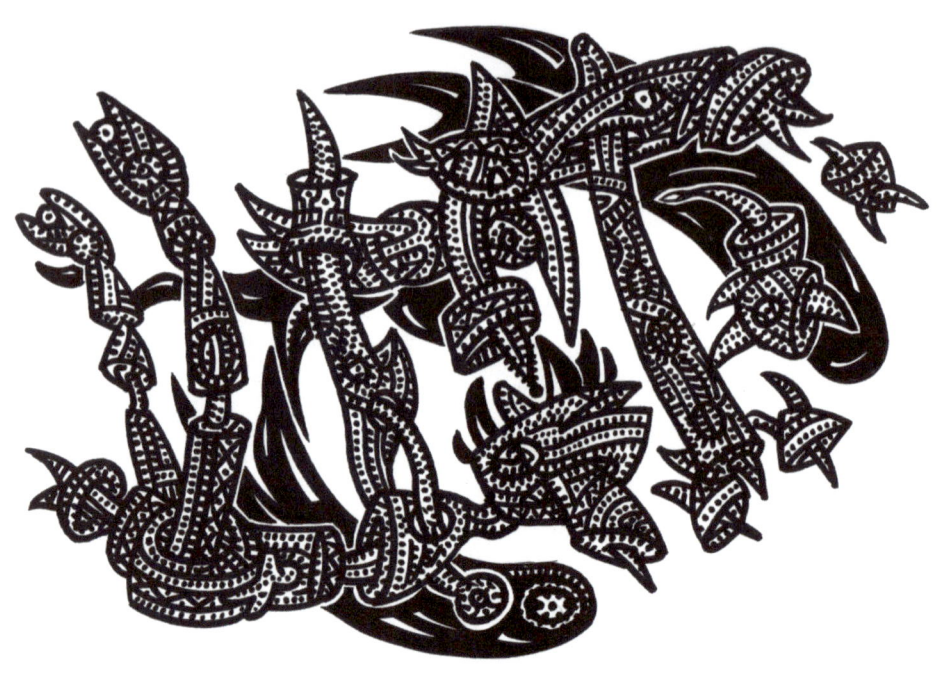

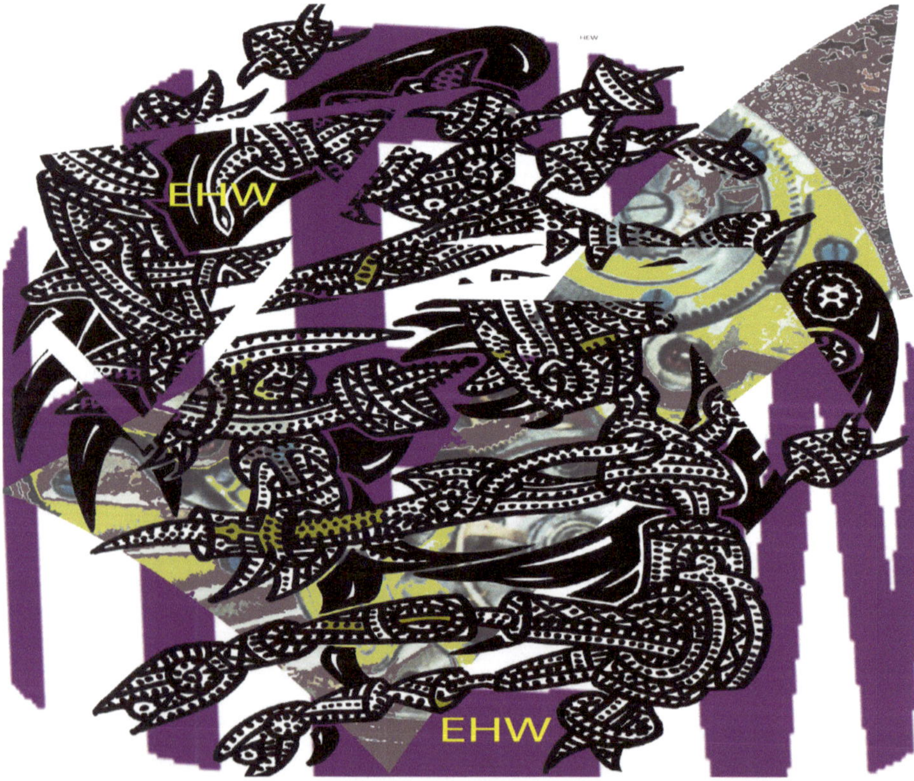

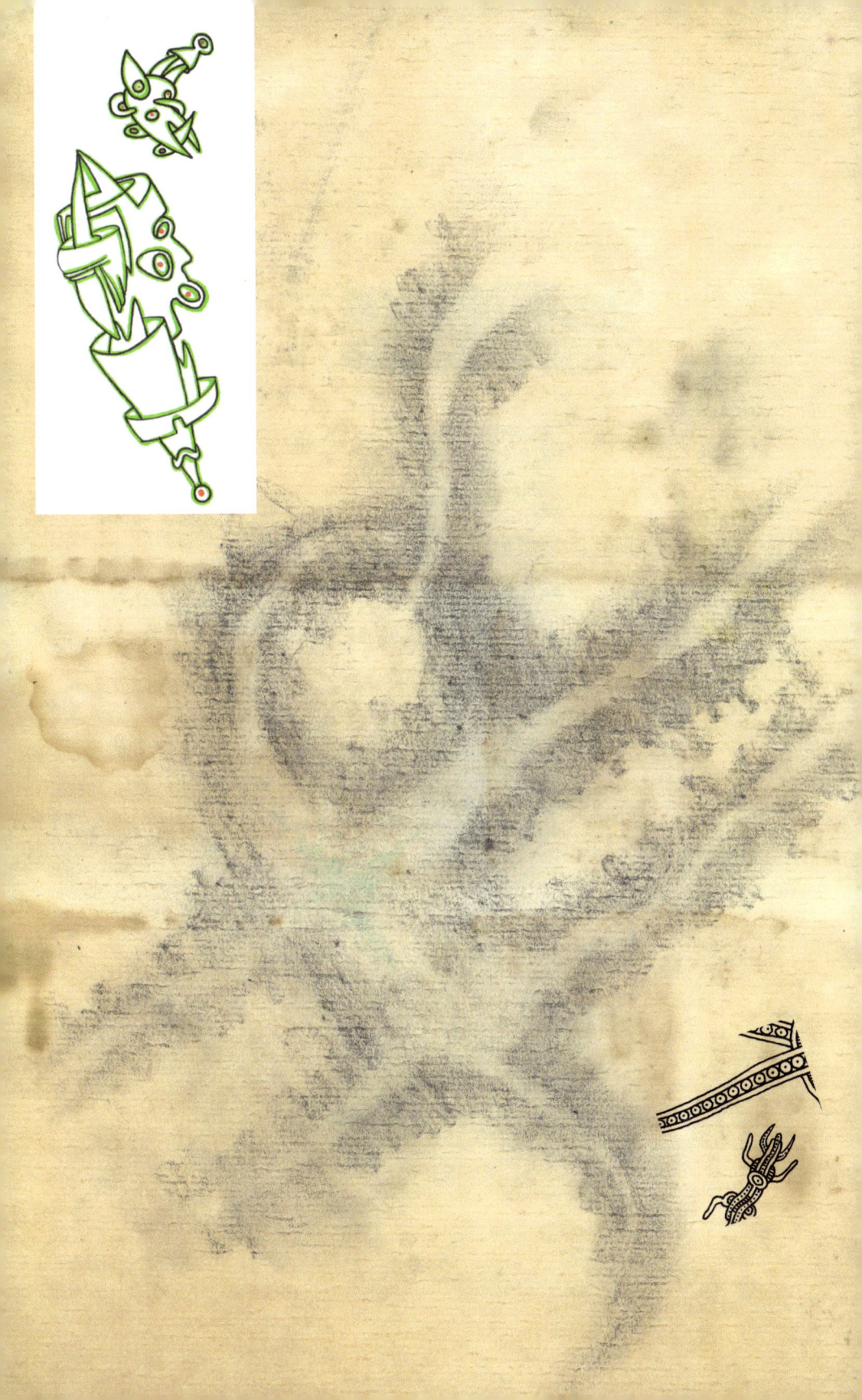

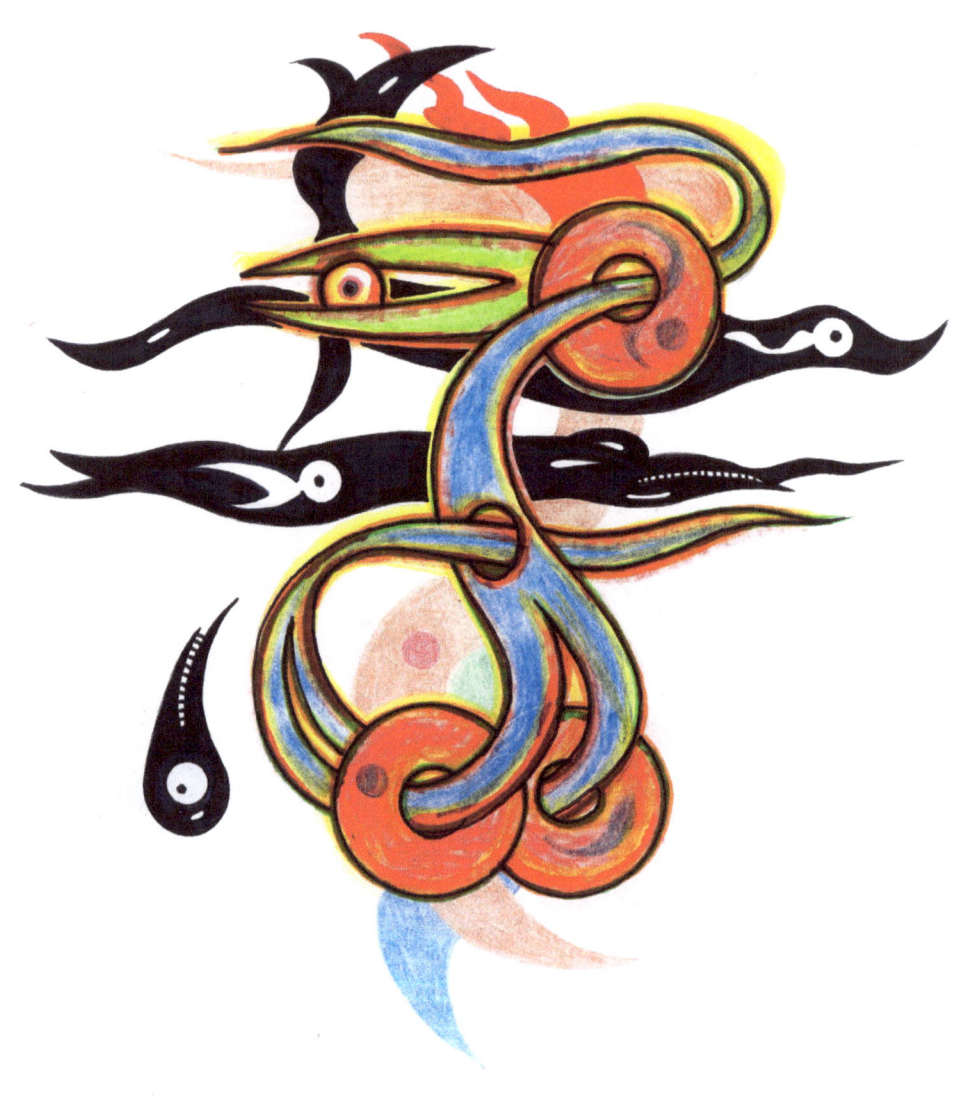

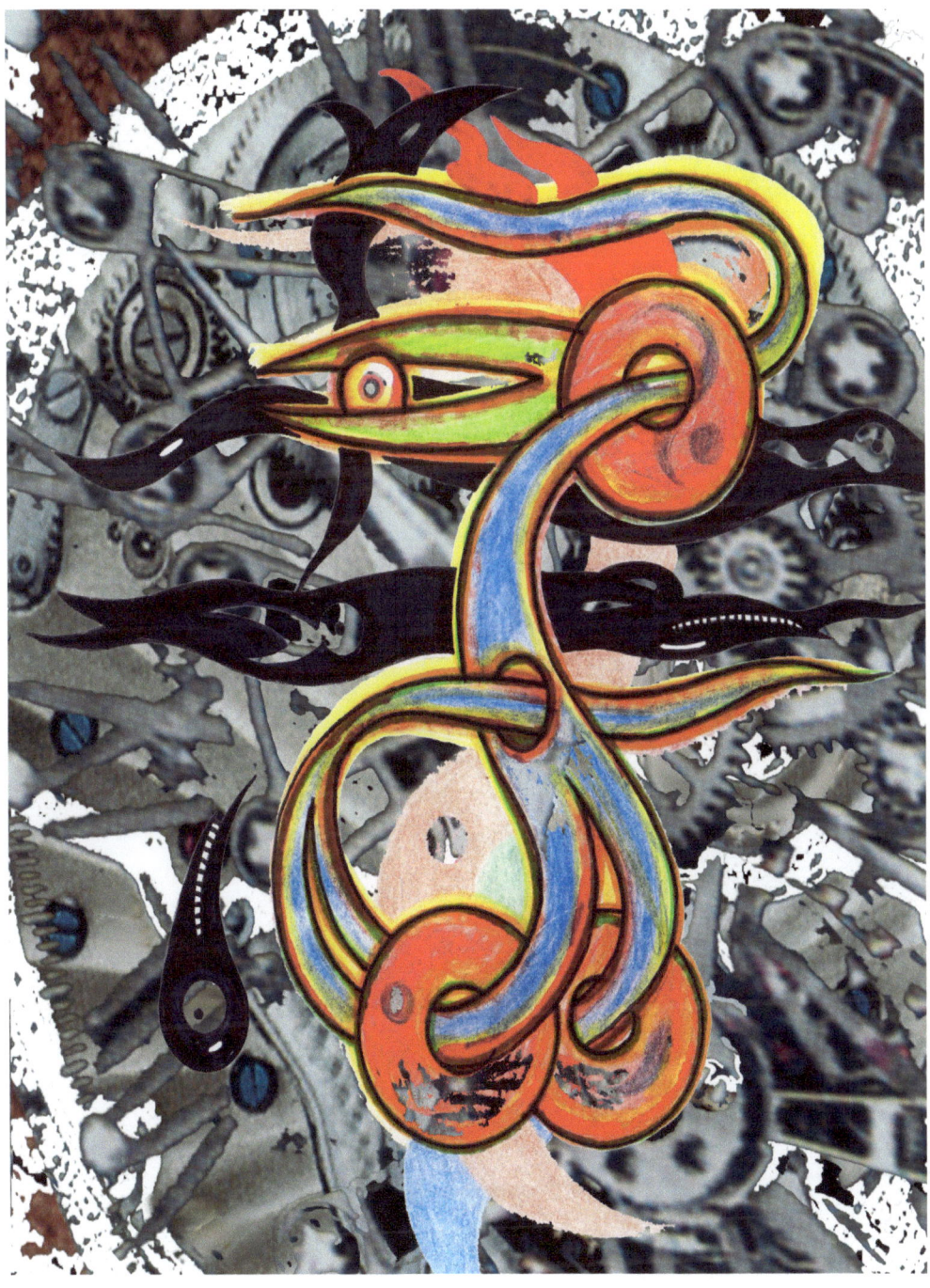

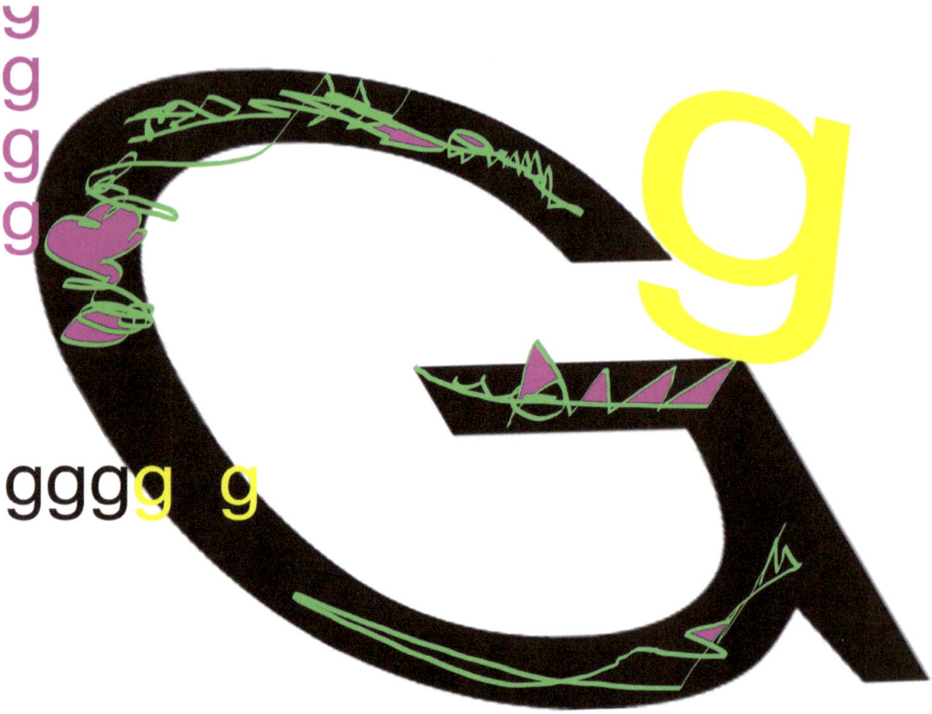

Gg
ggg g g

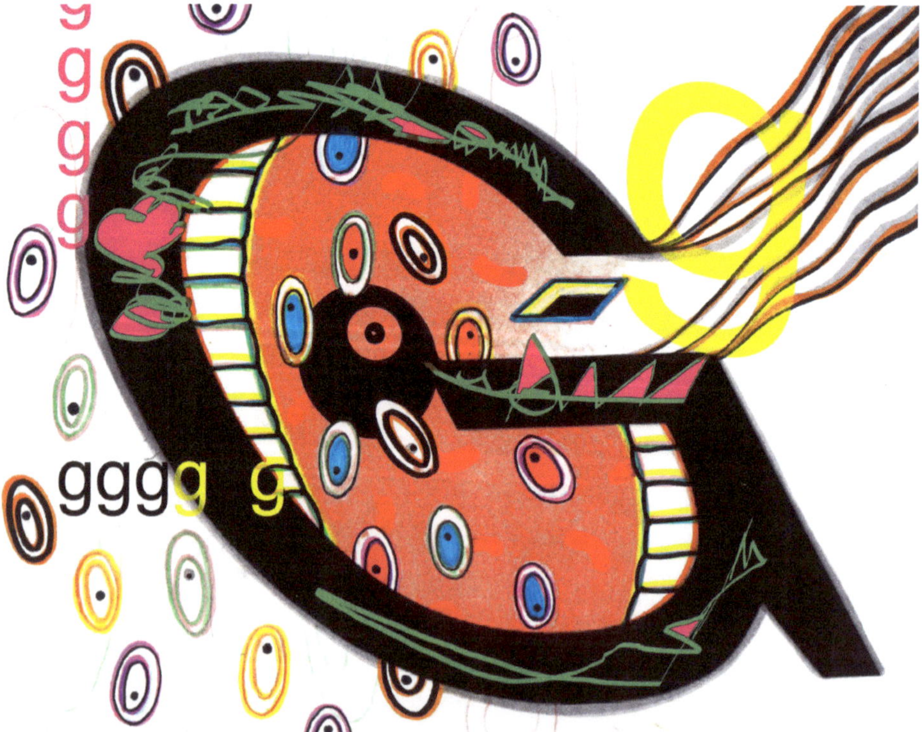

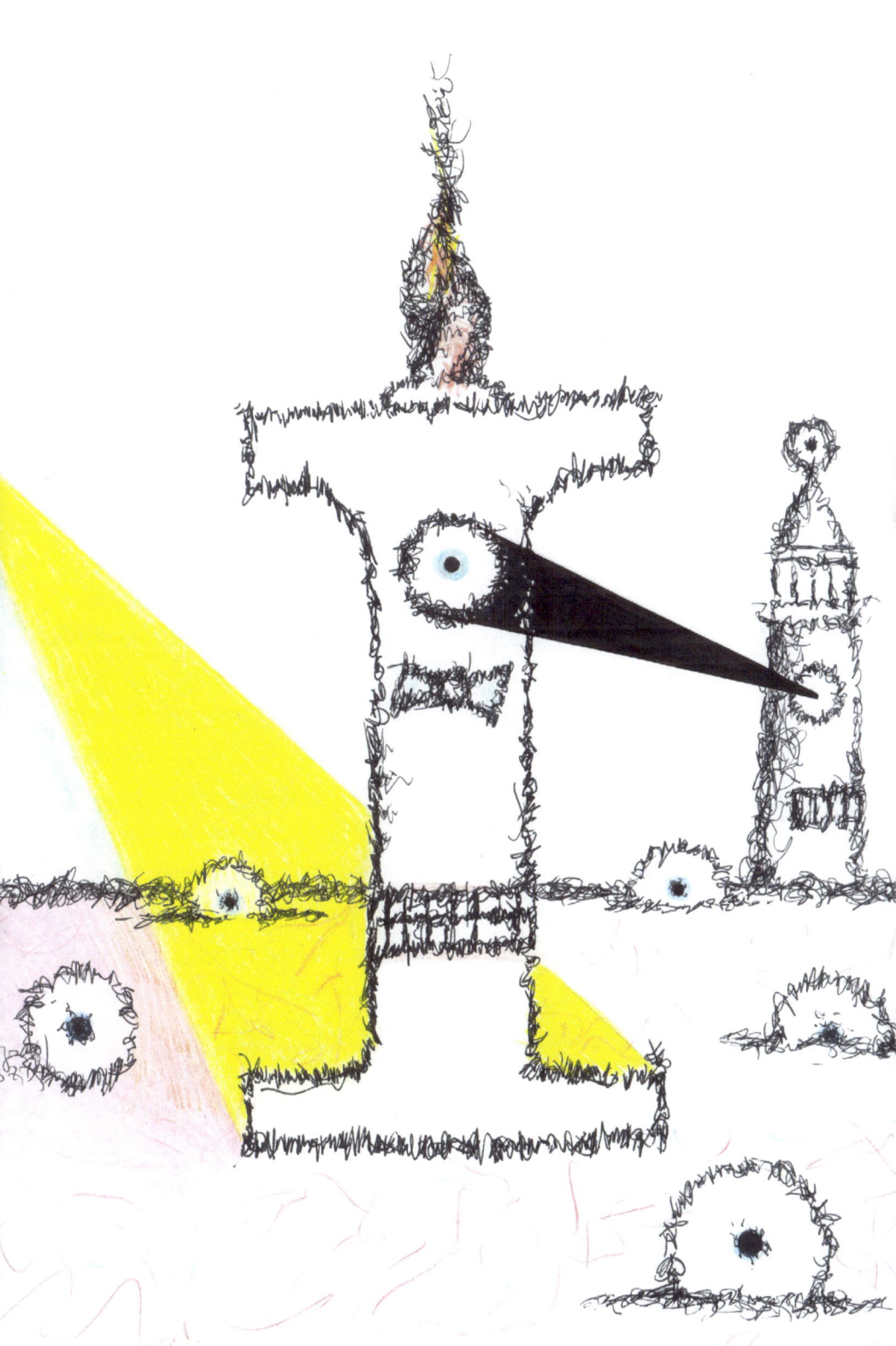

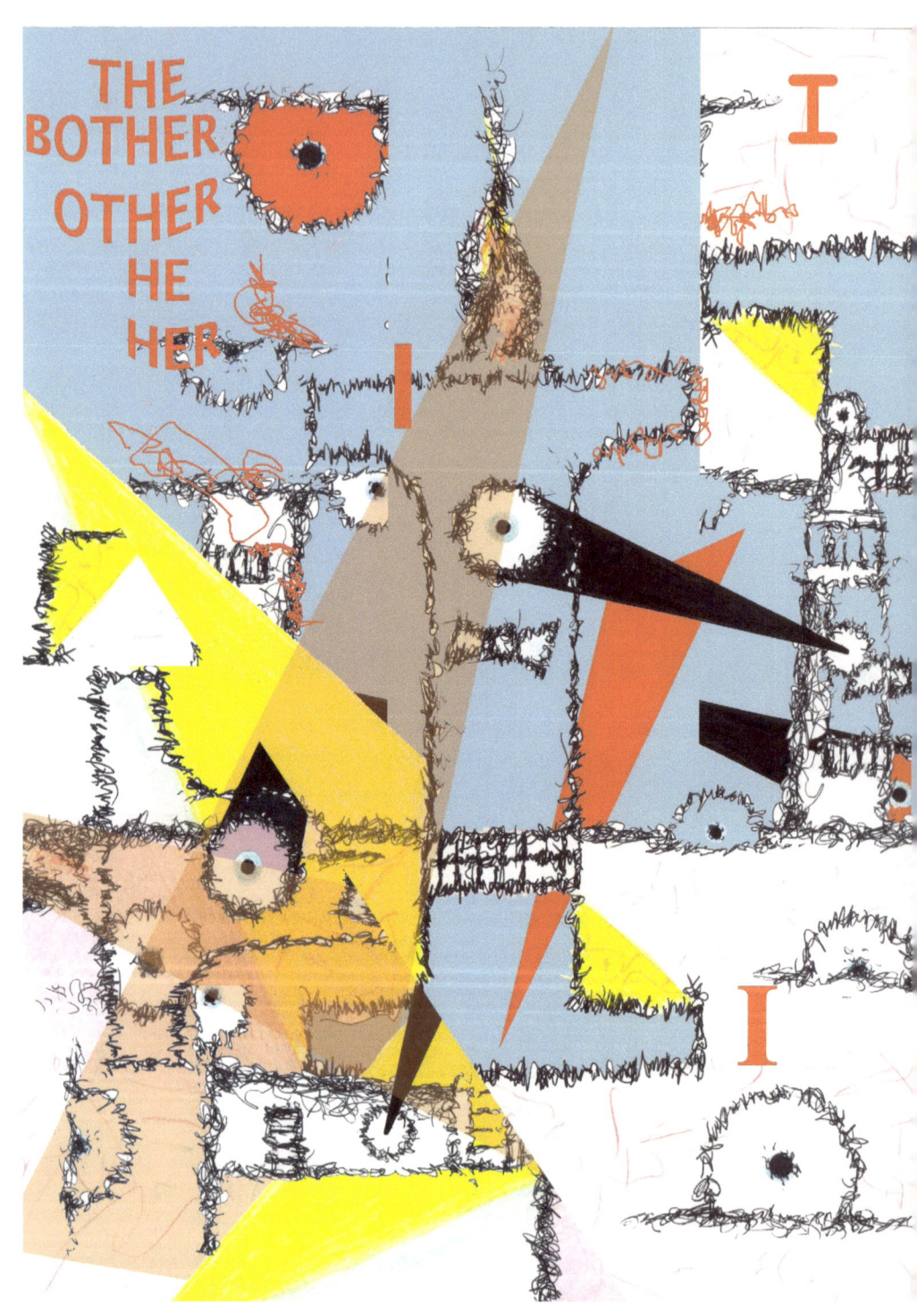

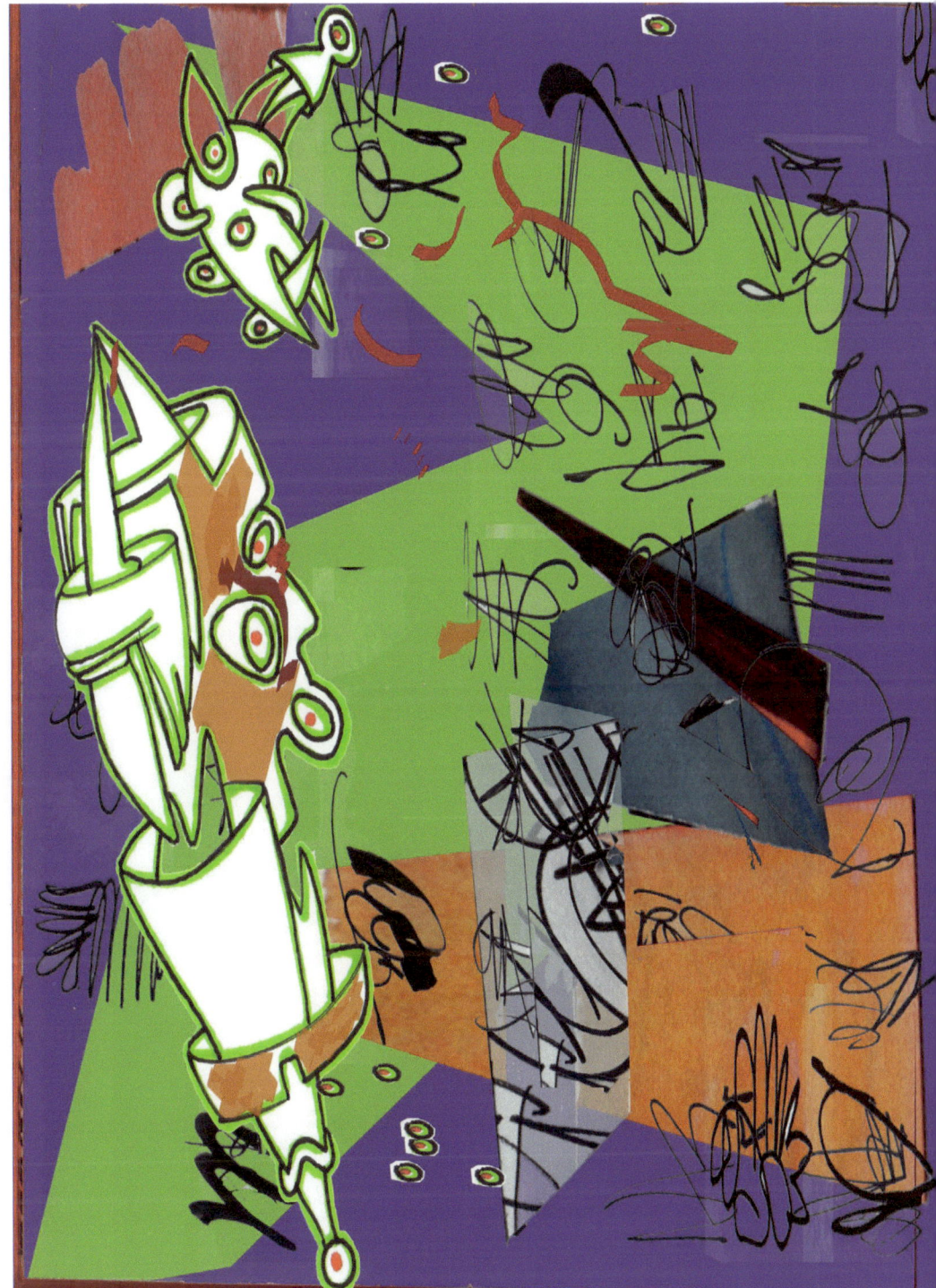

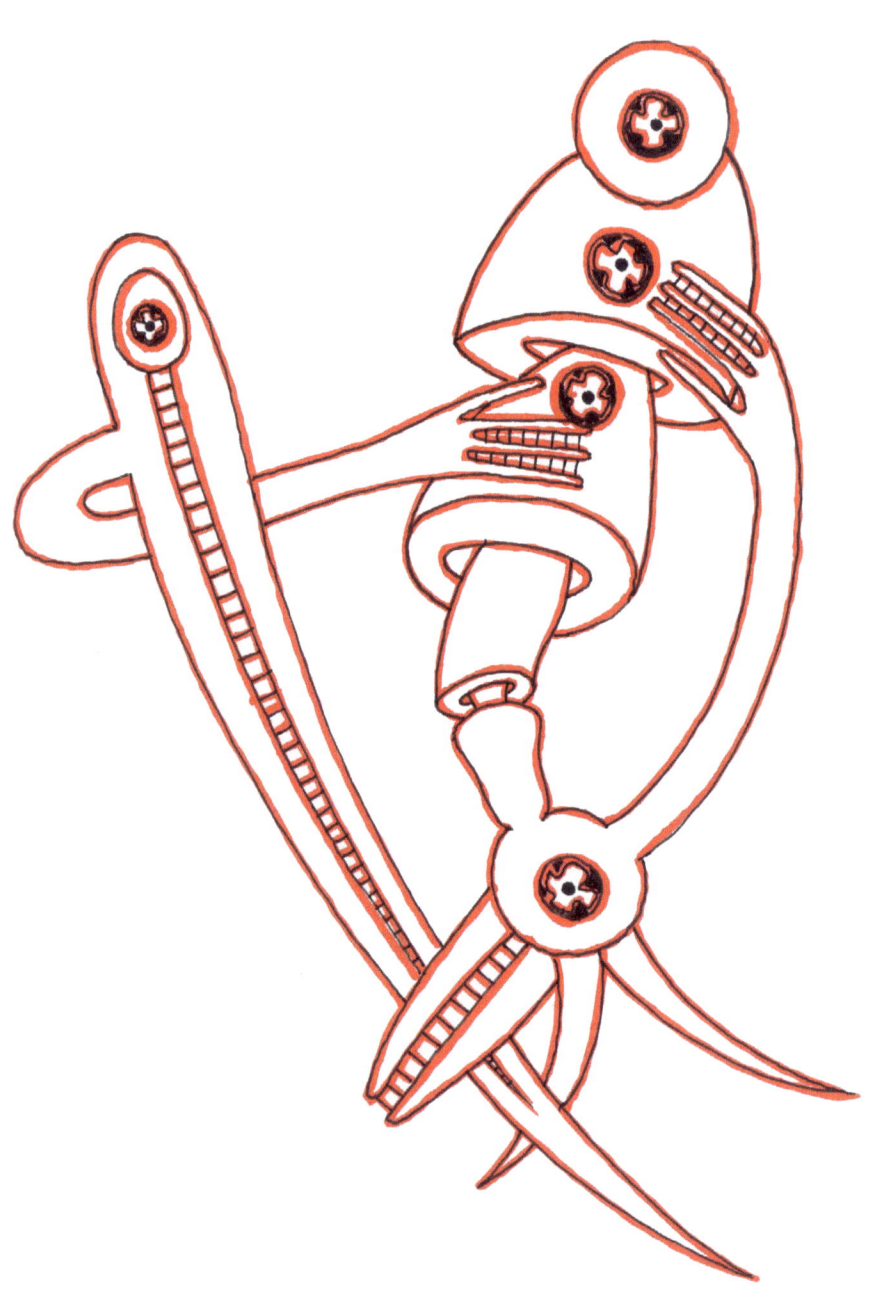

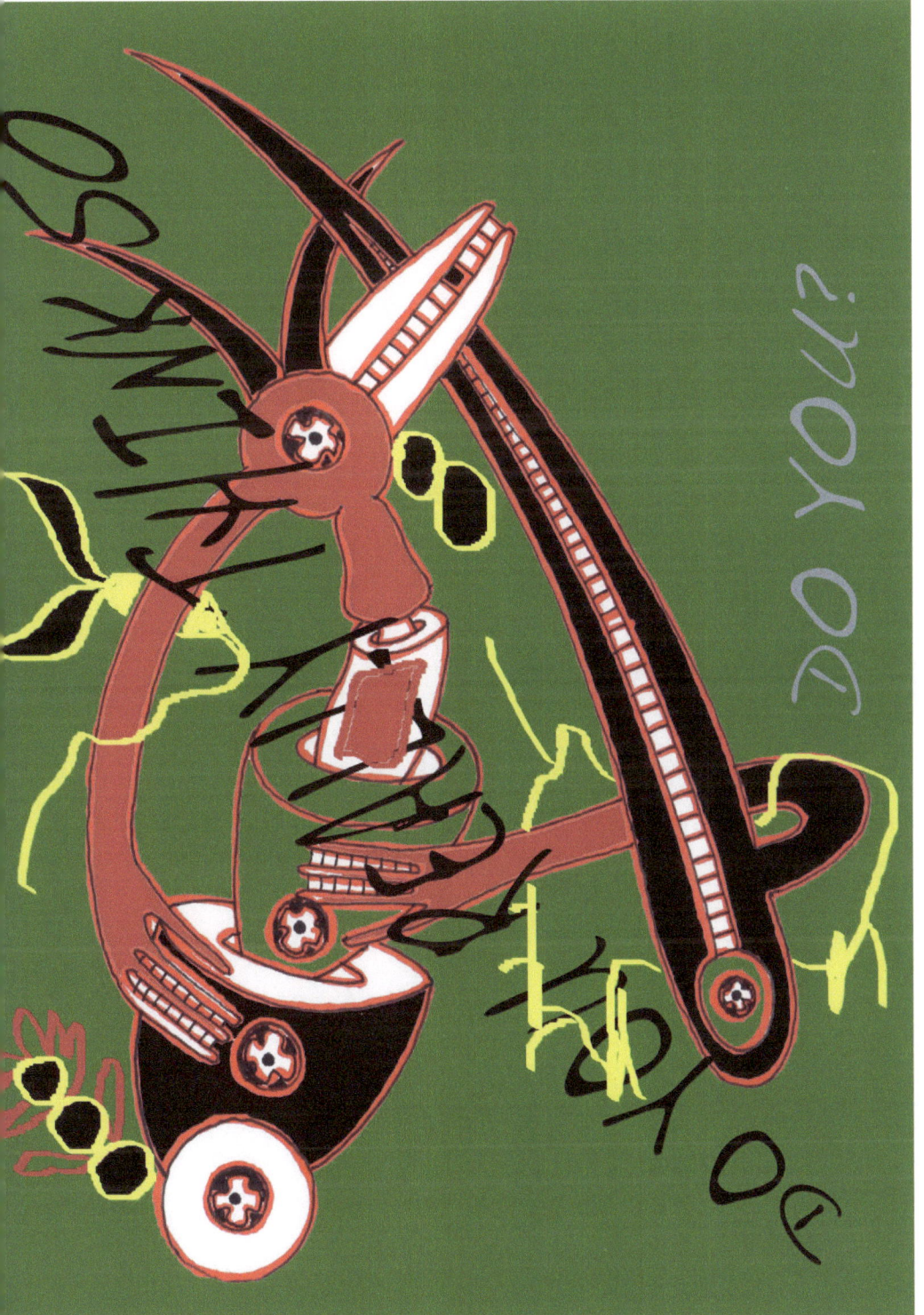

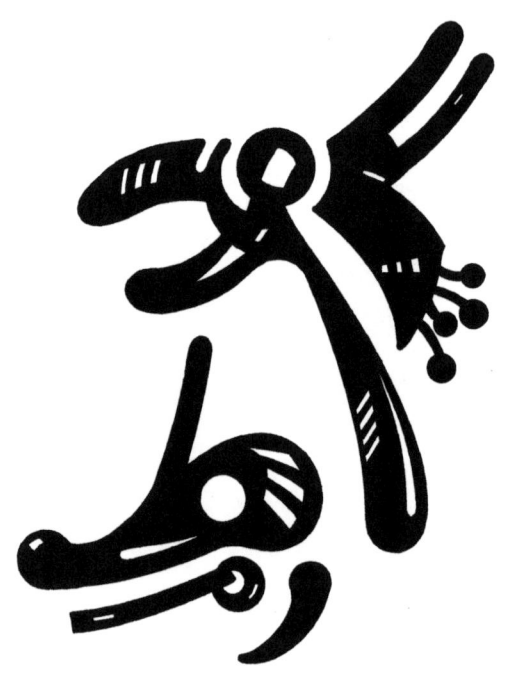

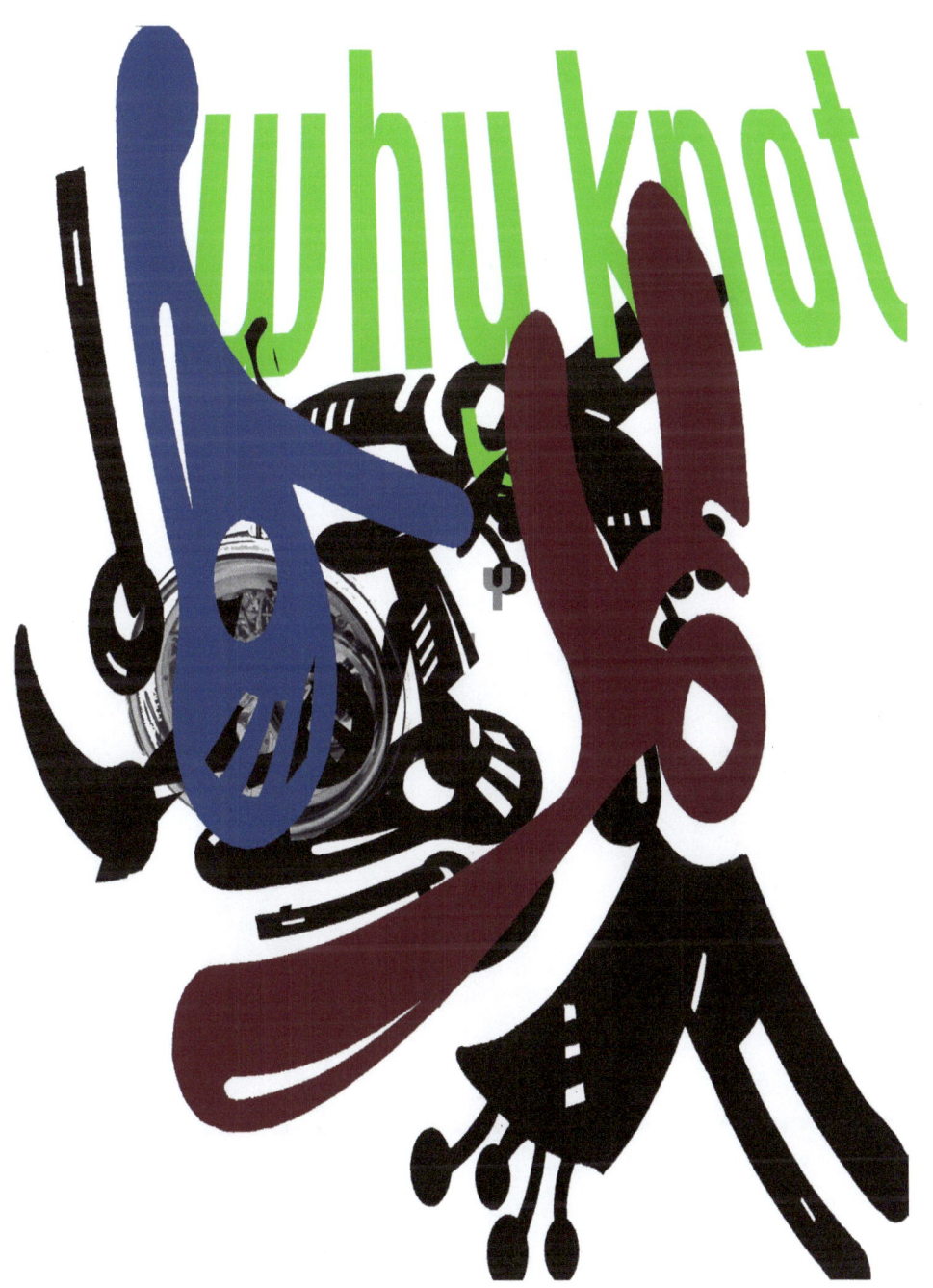

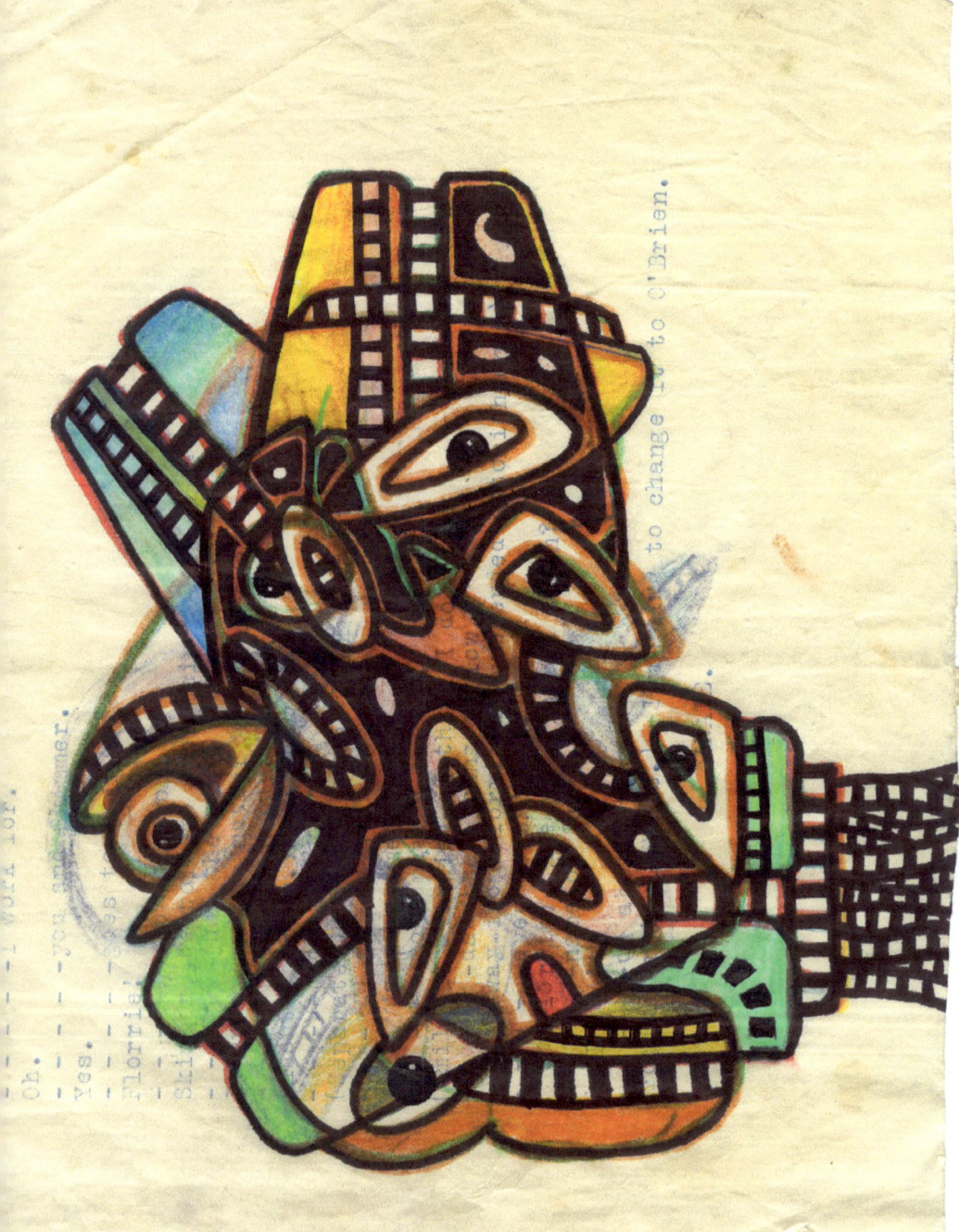

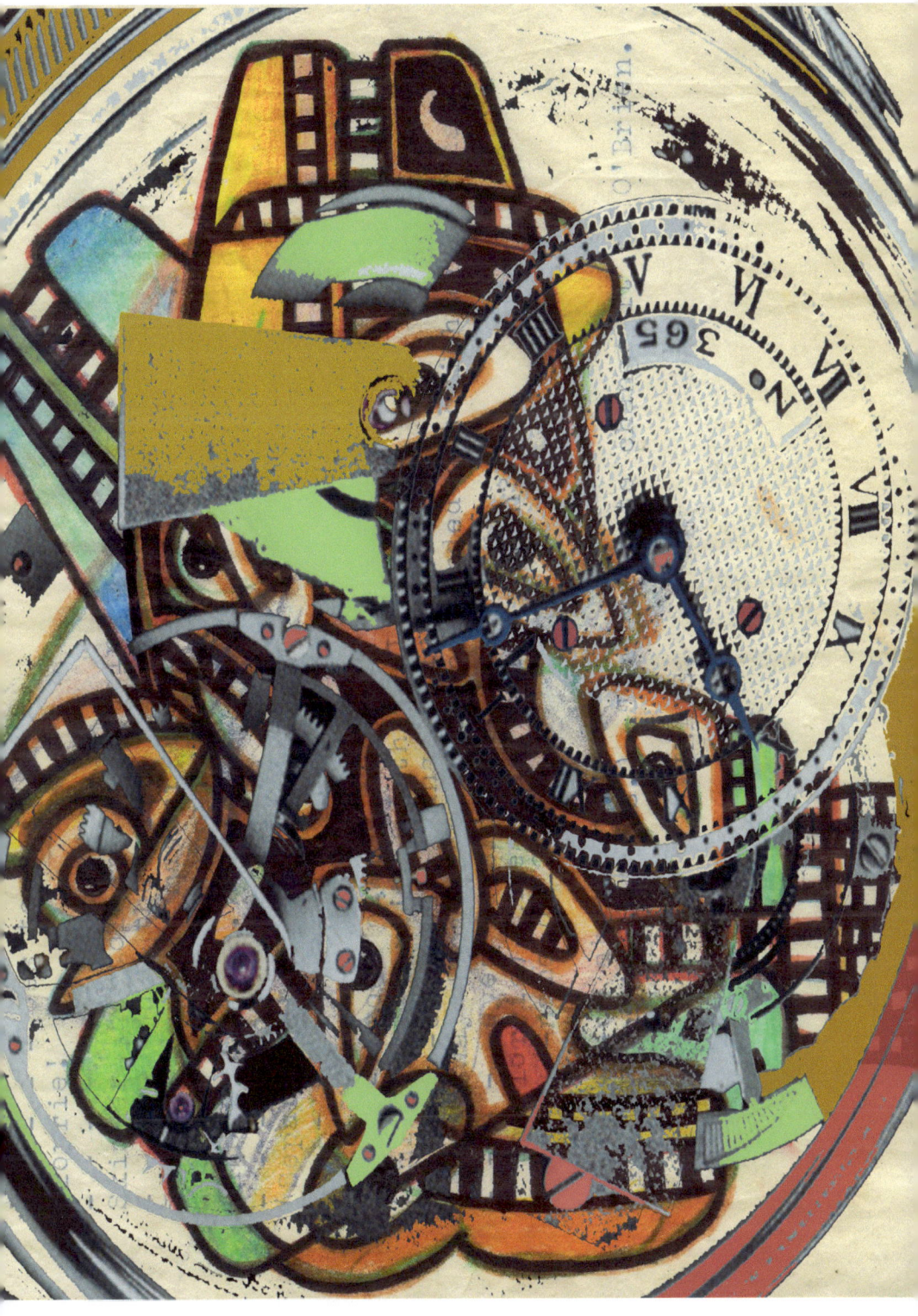

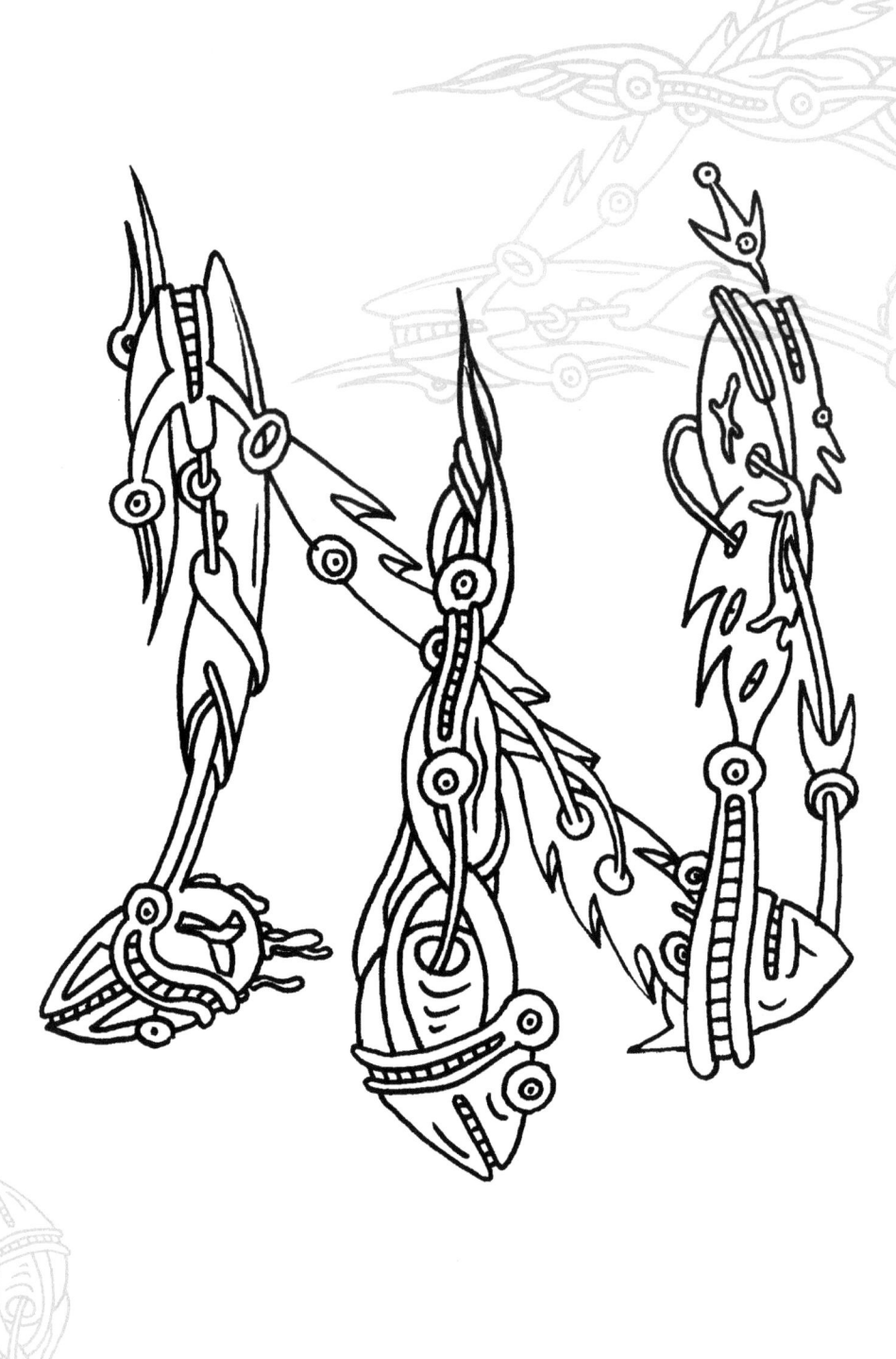

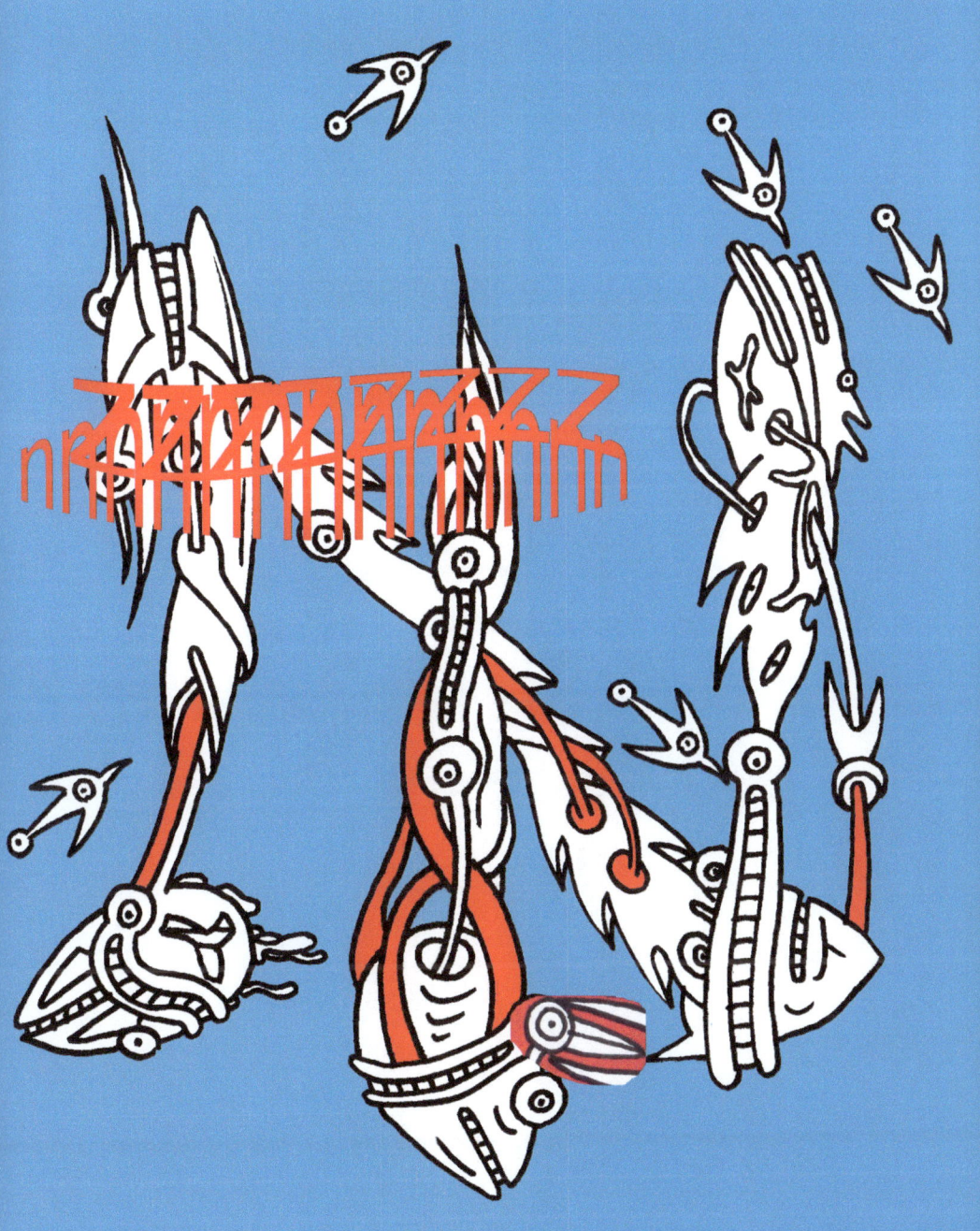

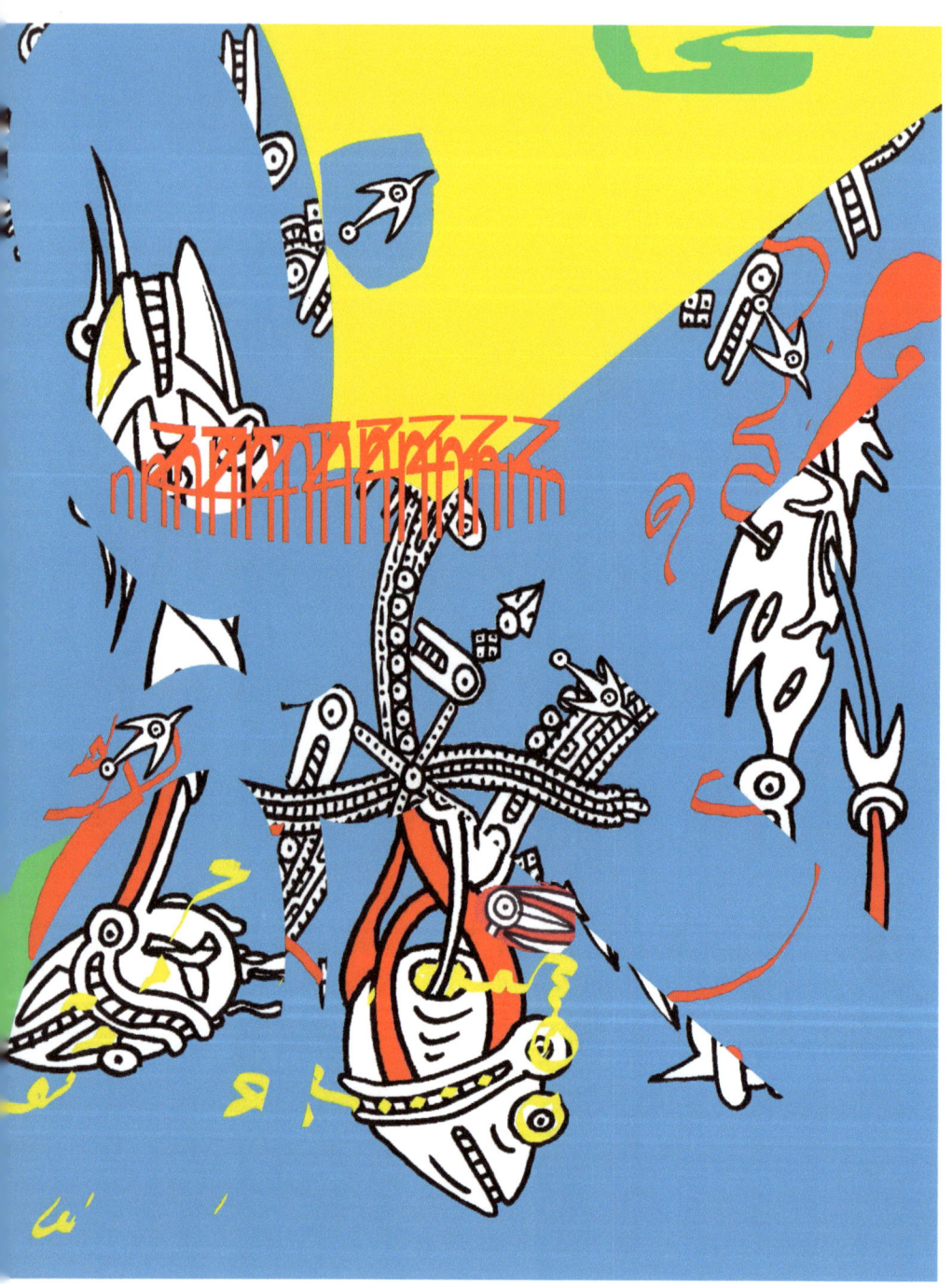

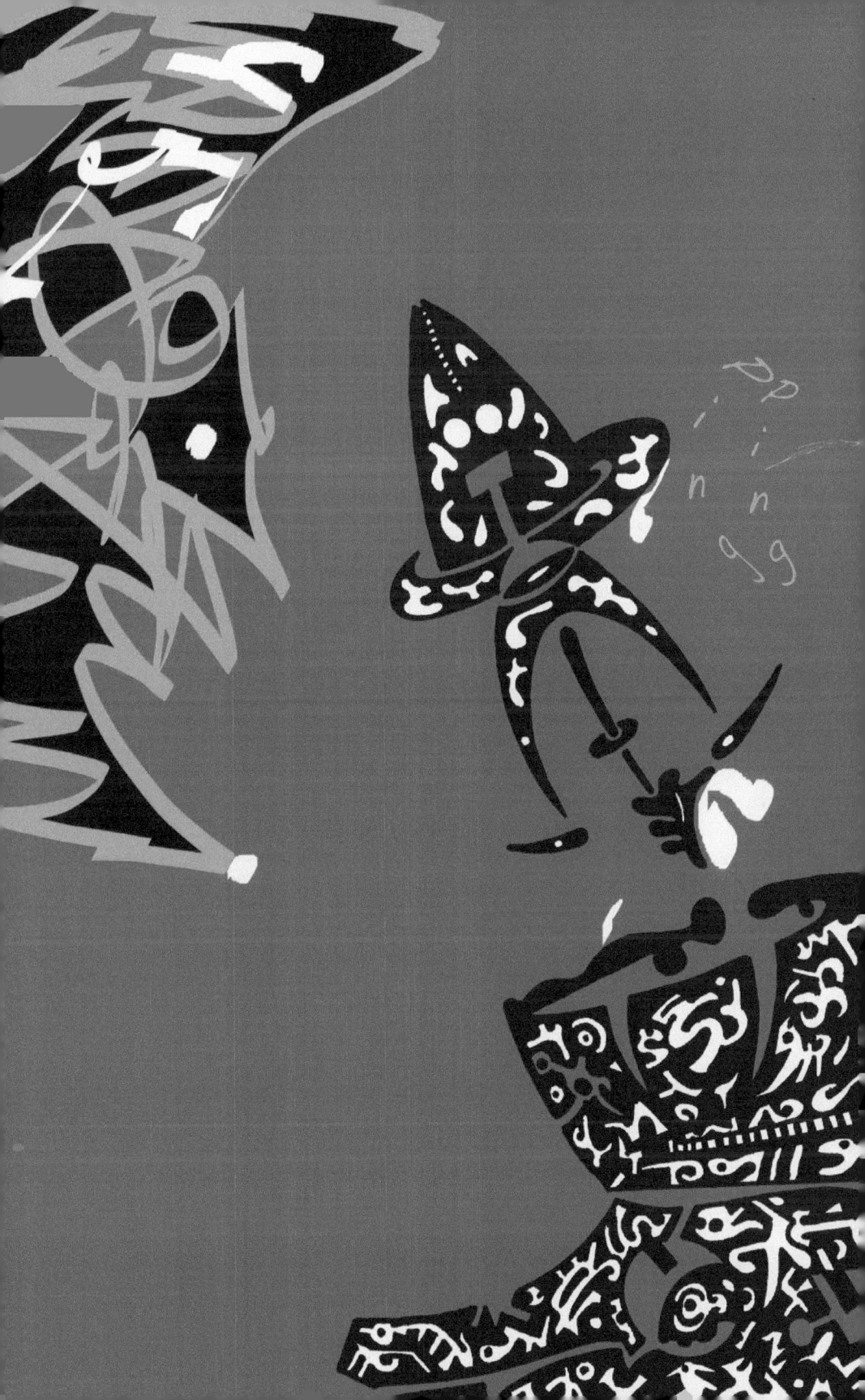

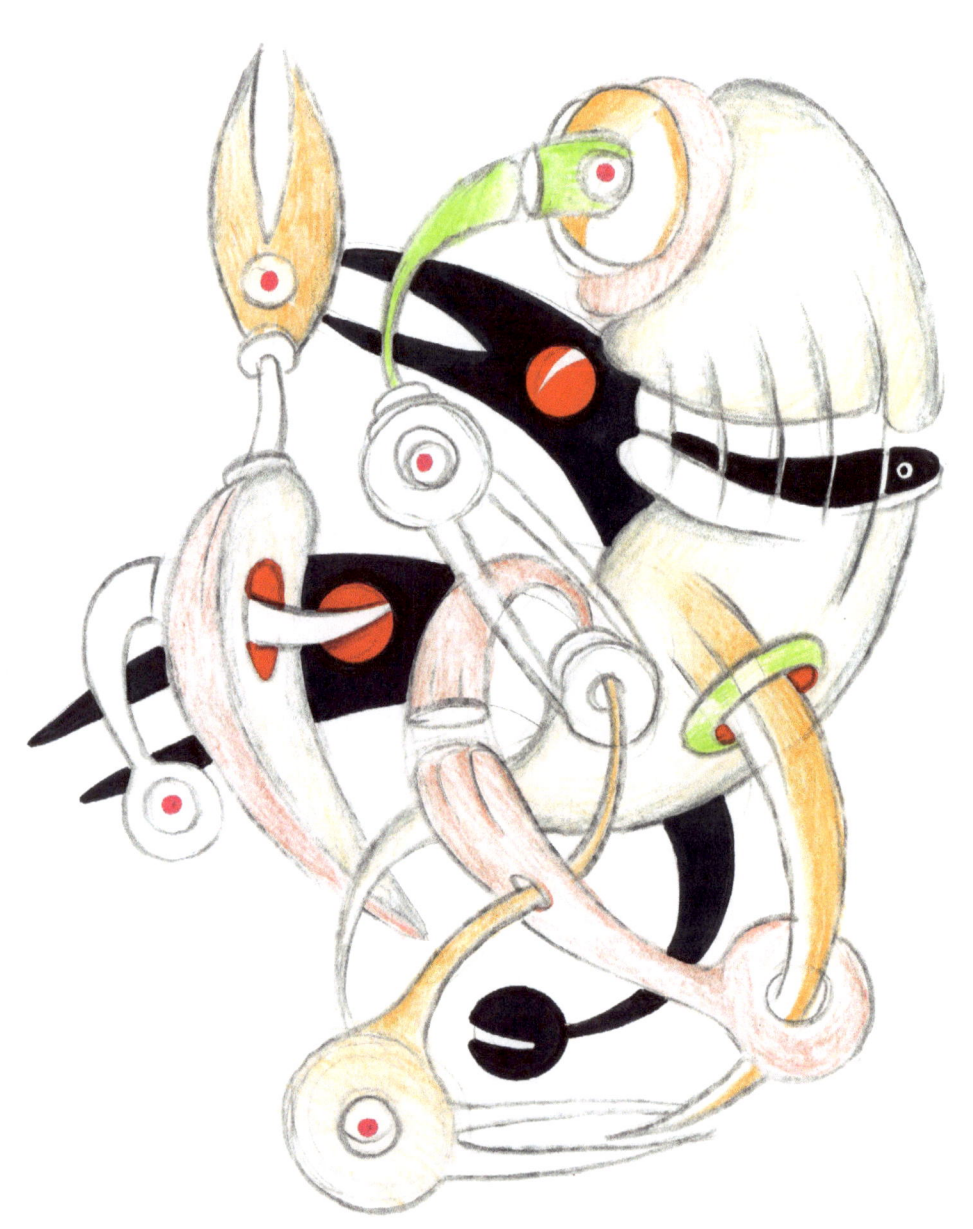

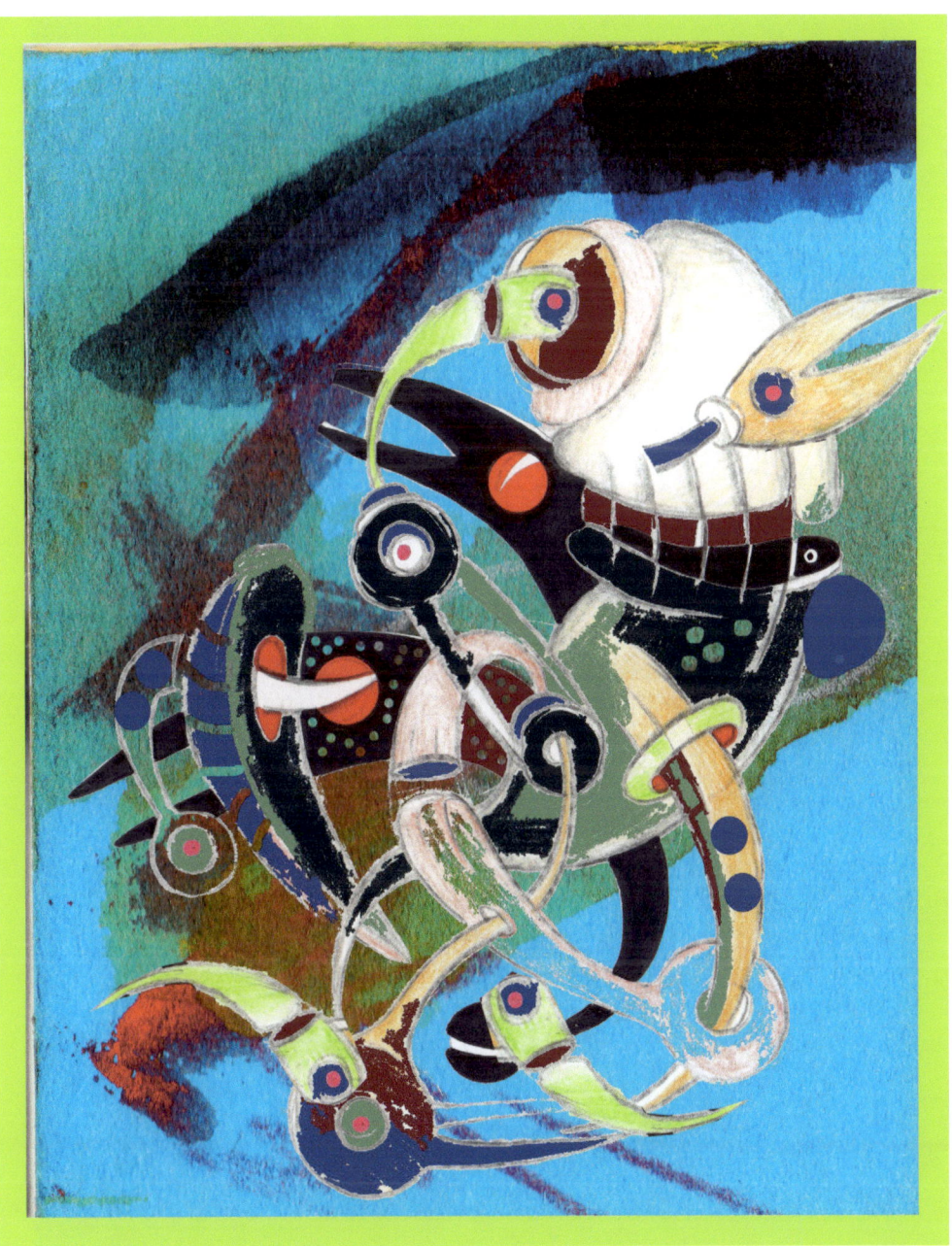

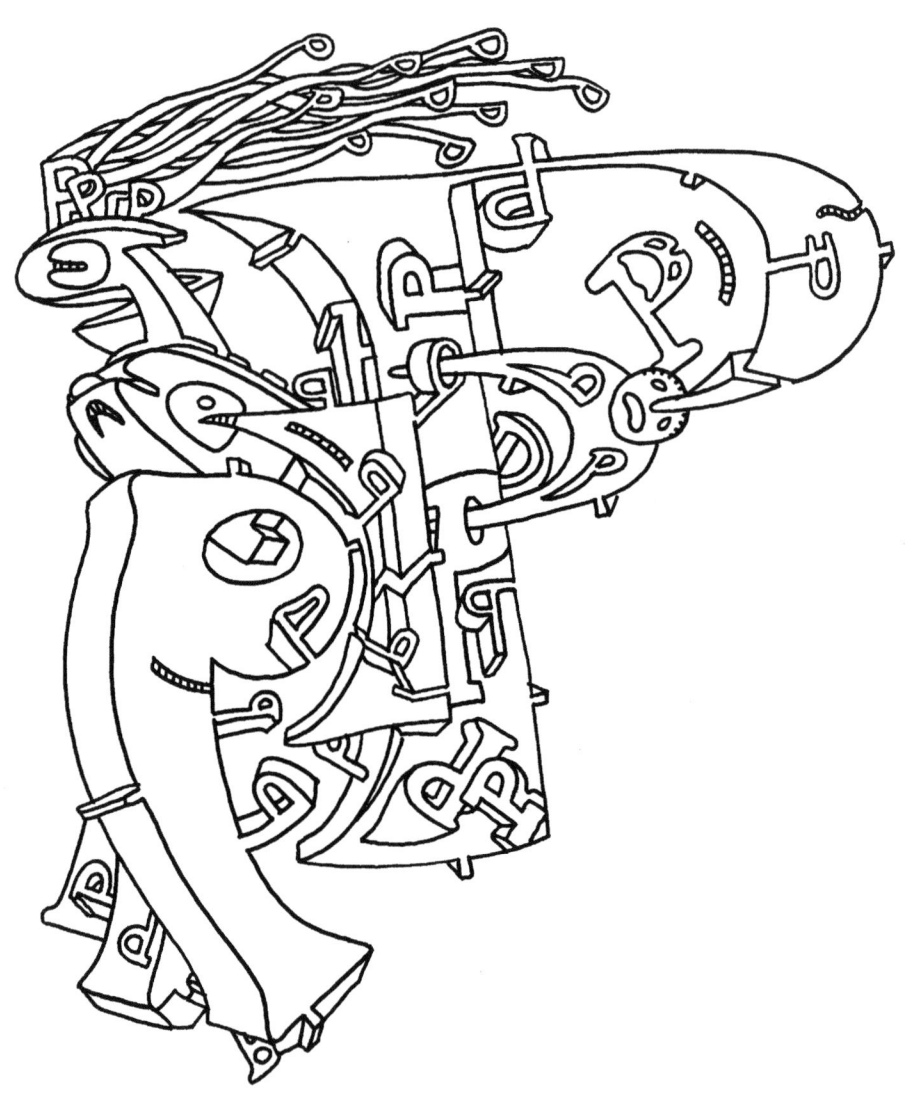

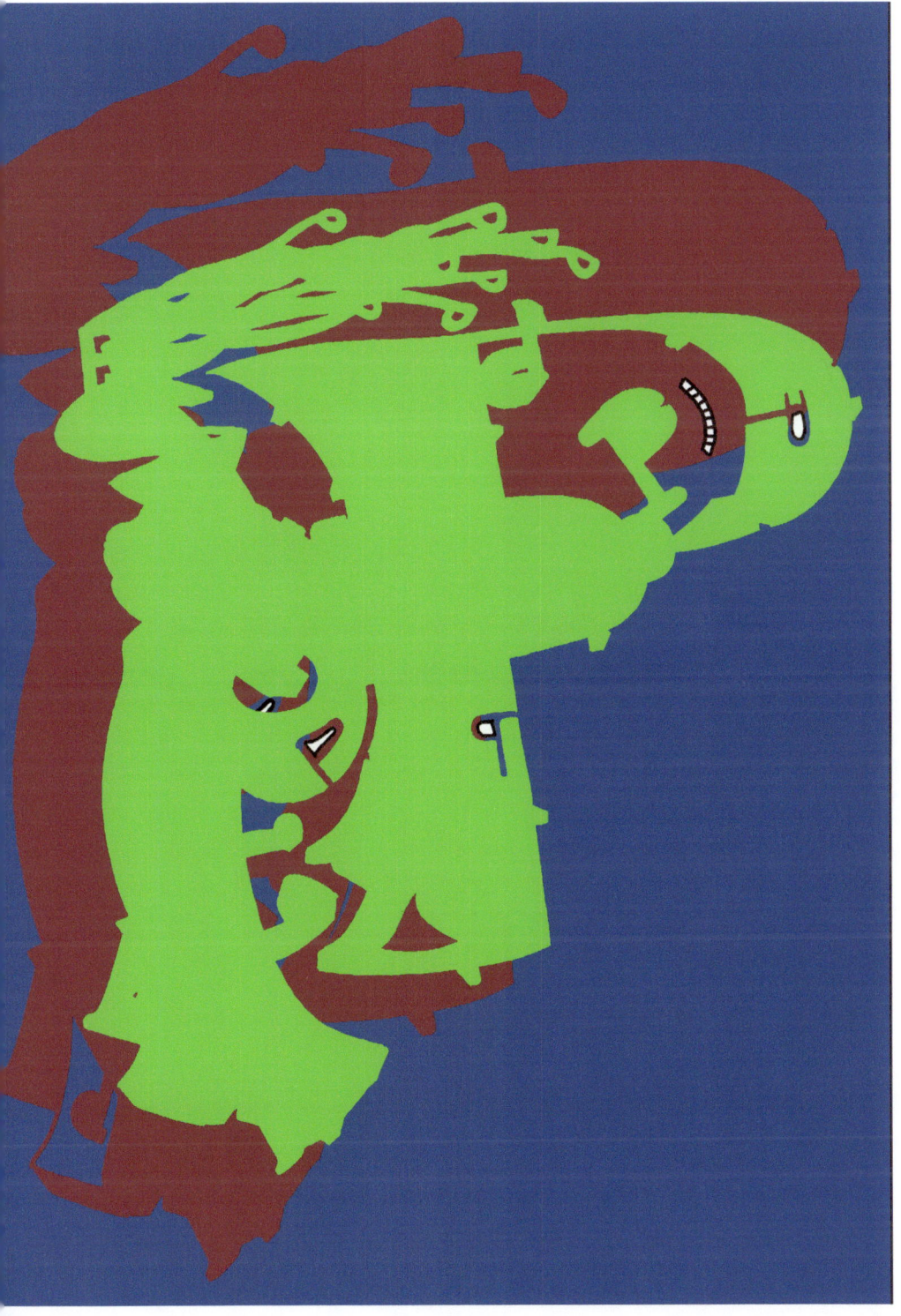

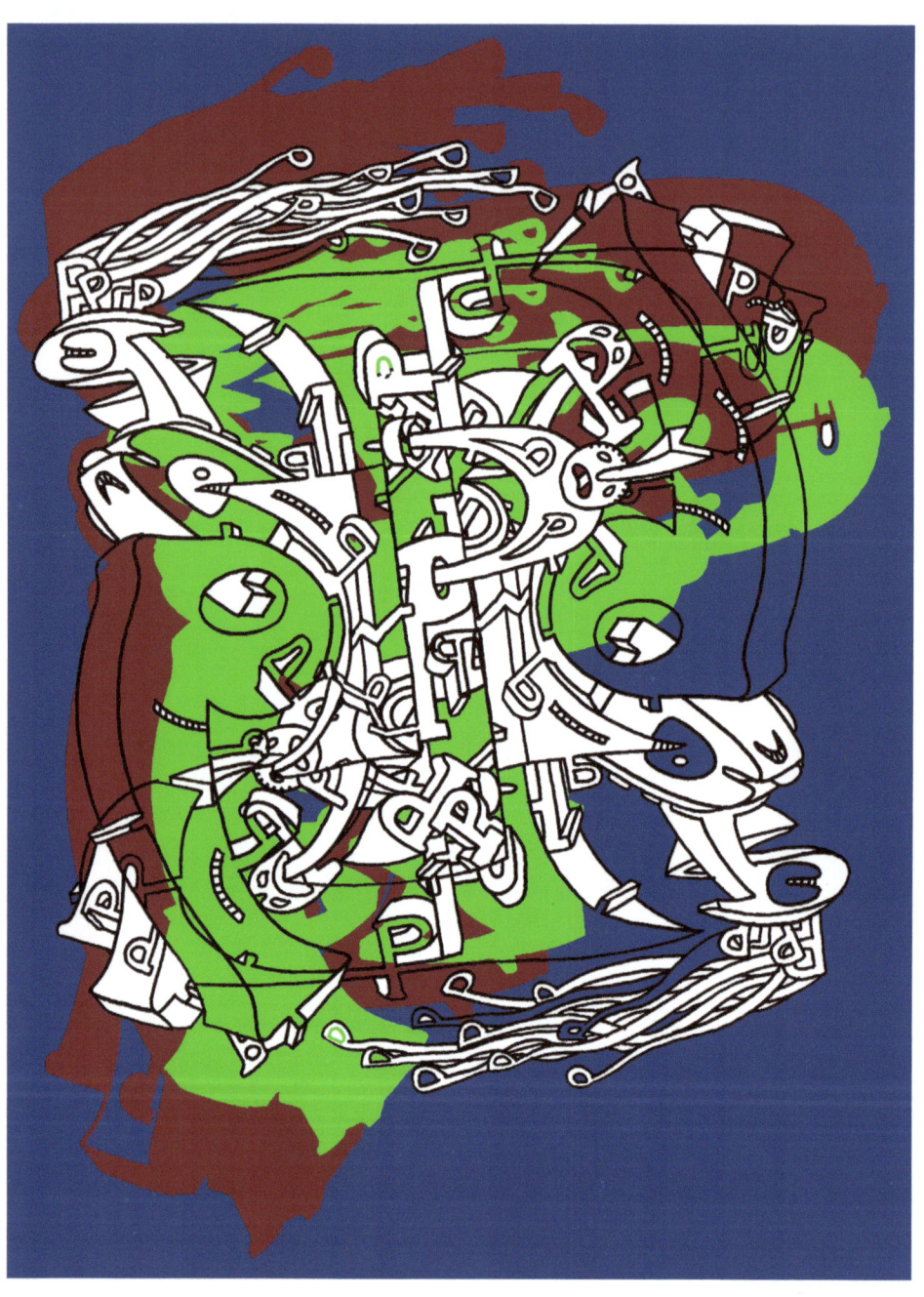

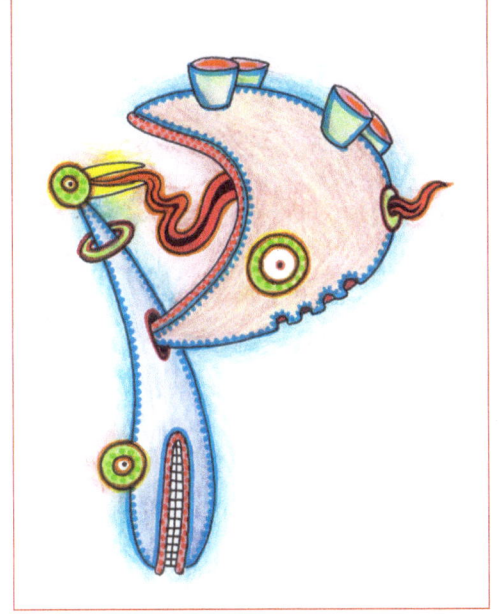

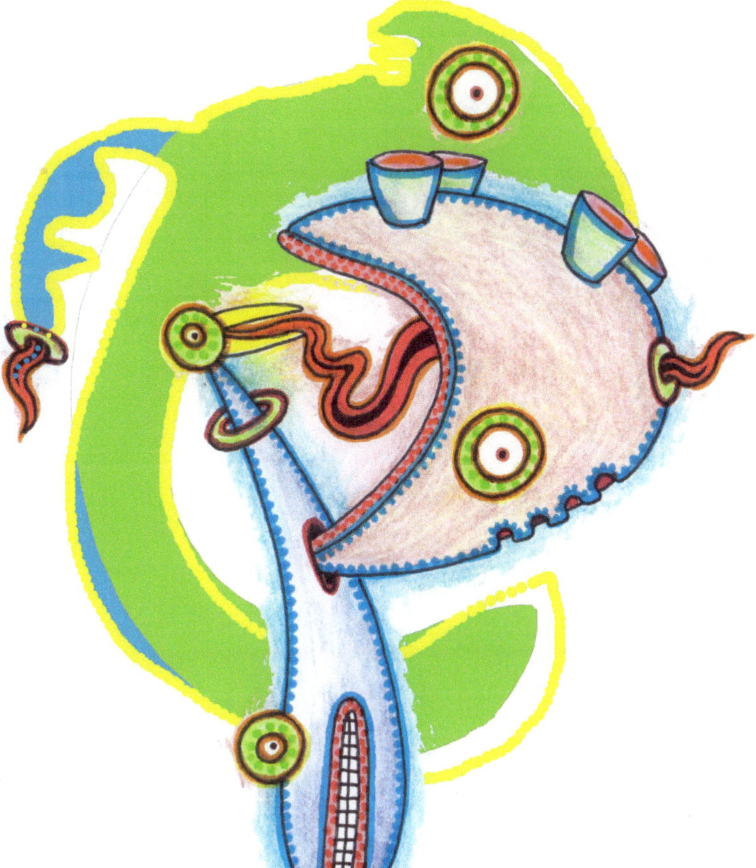

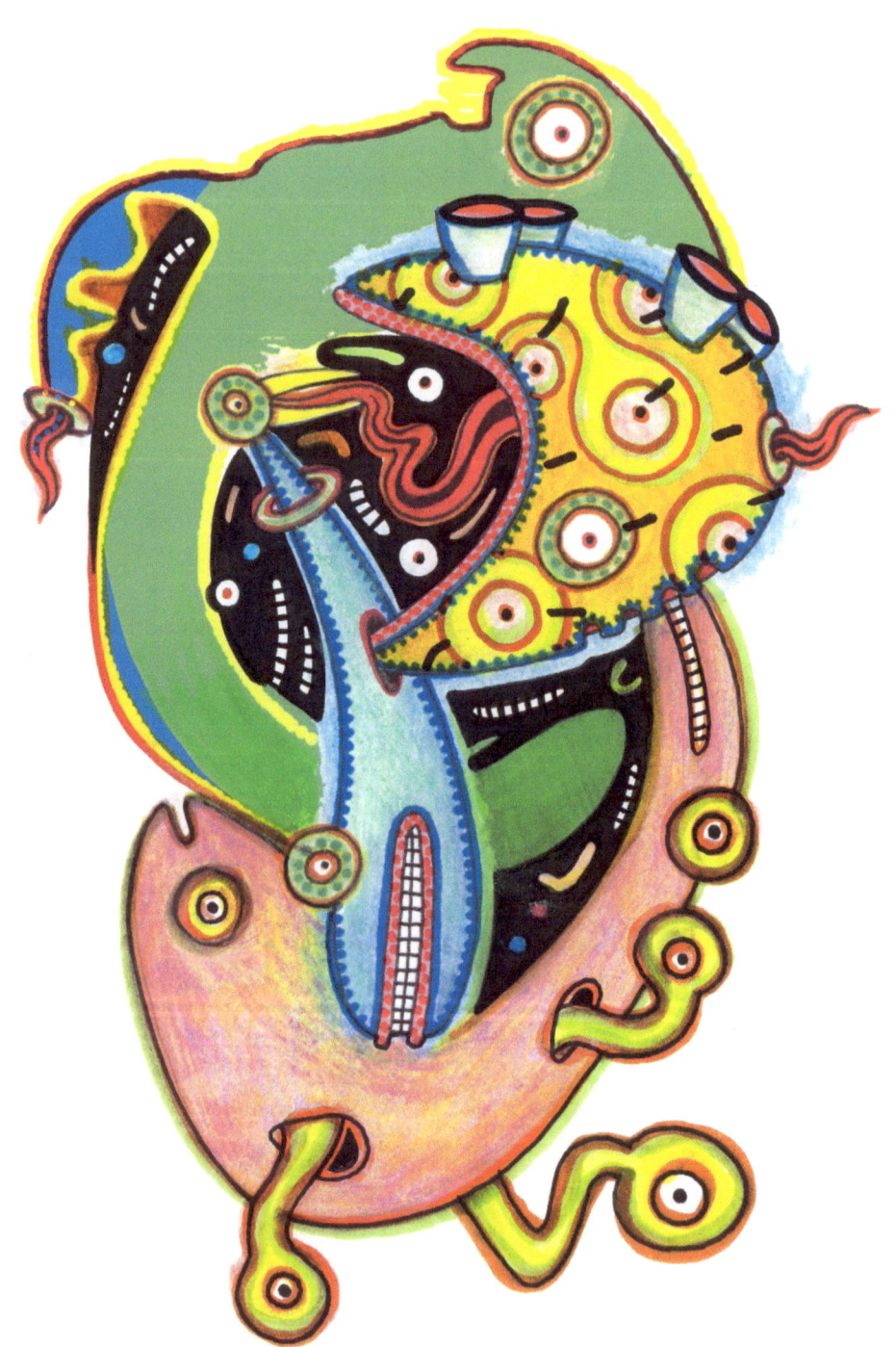

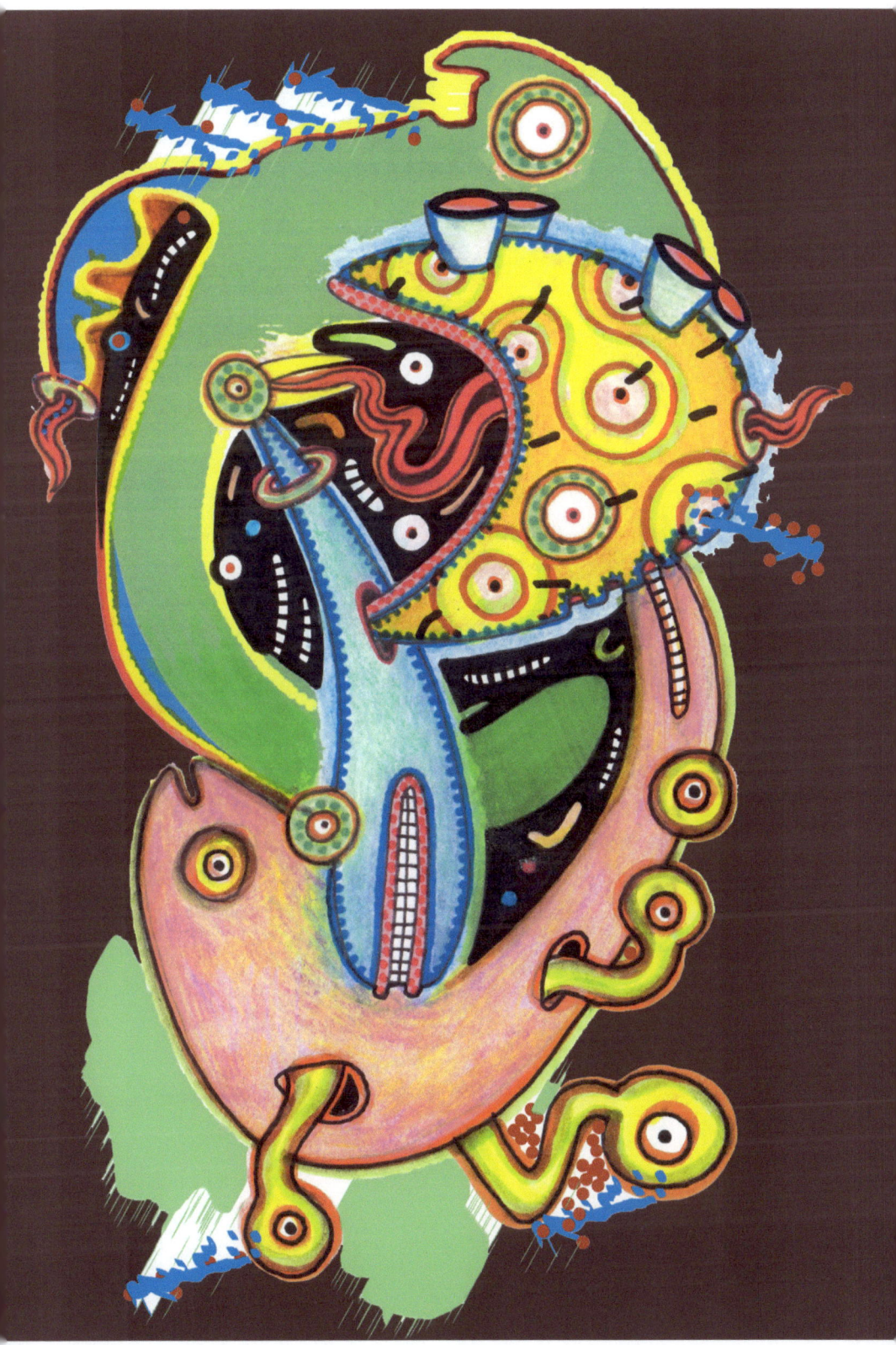

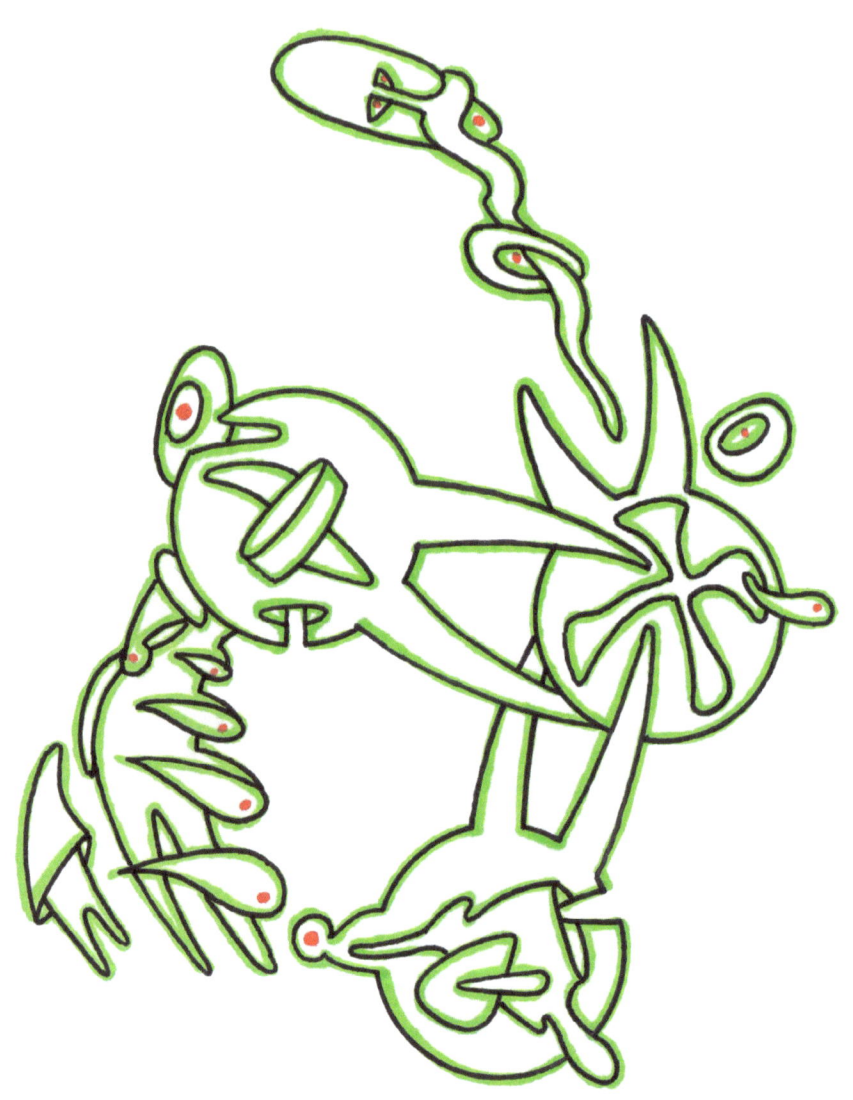

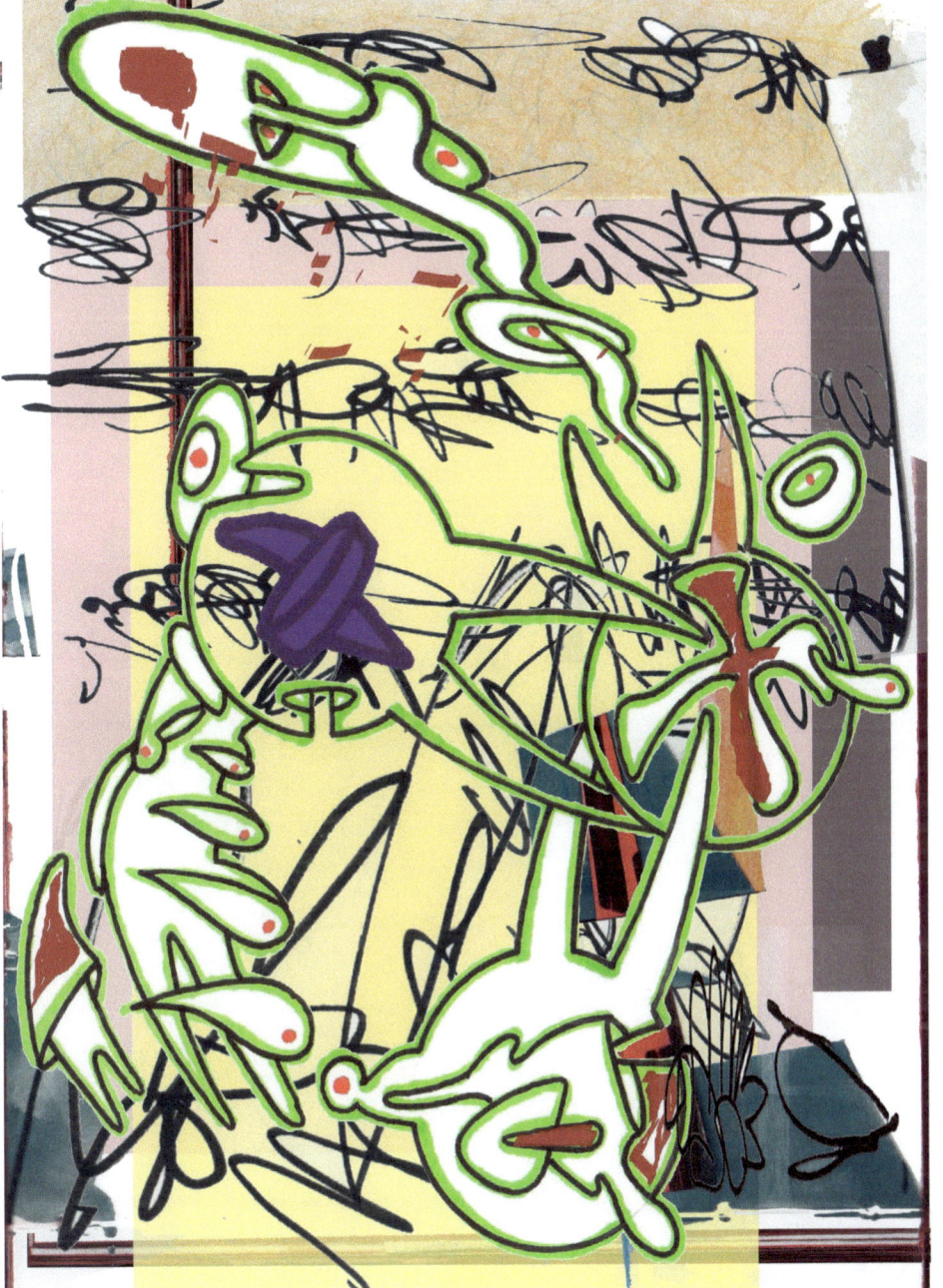

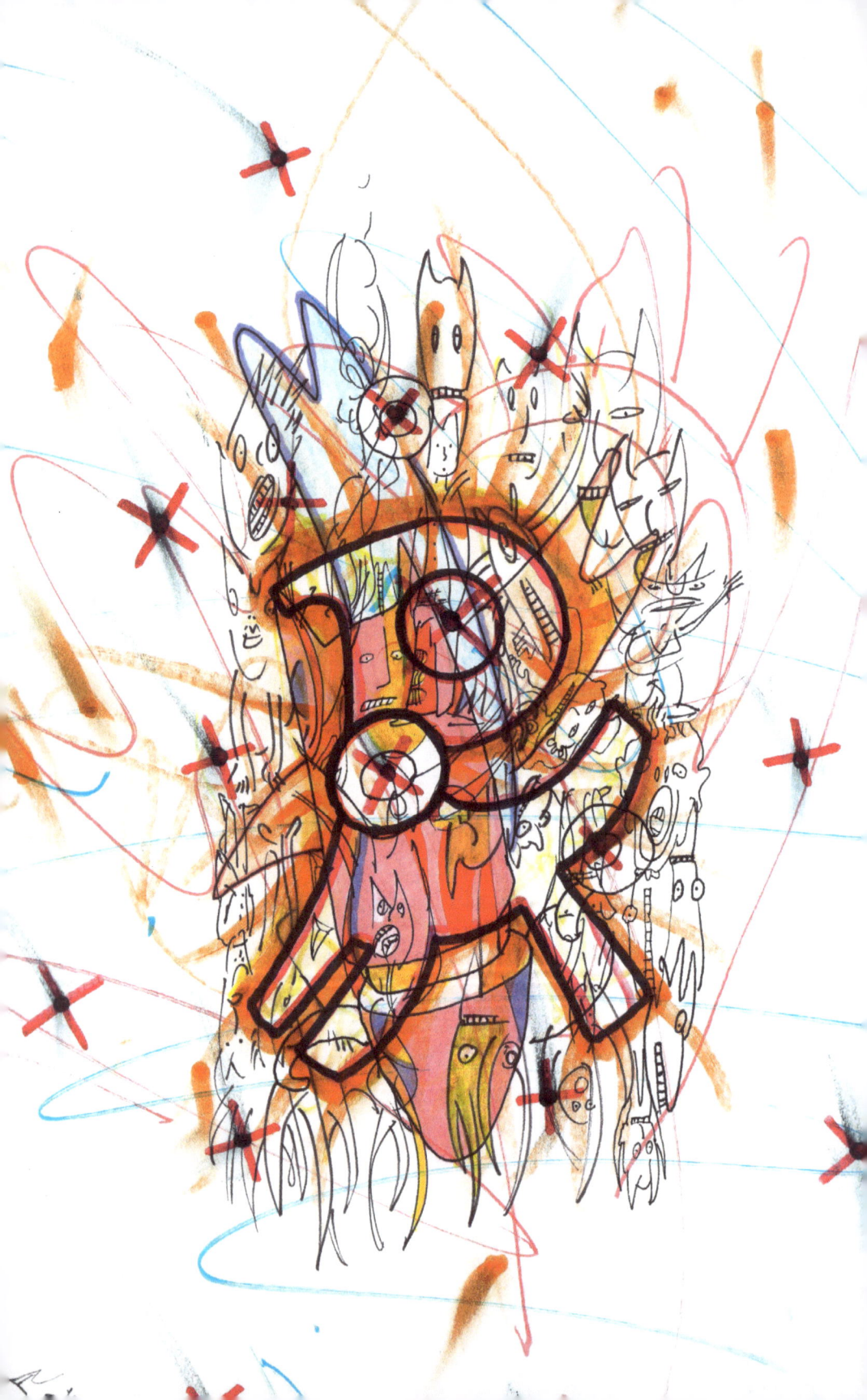

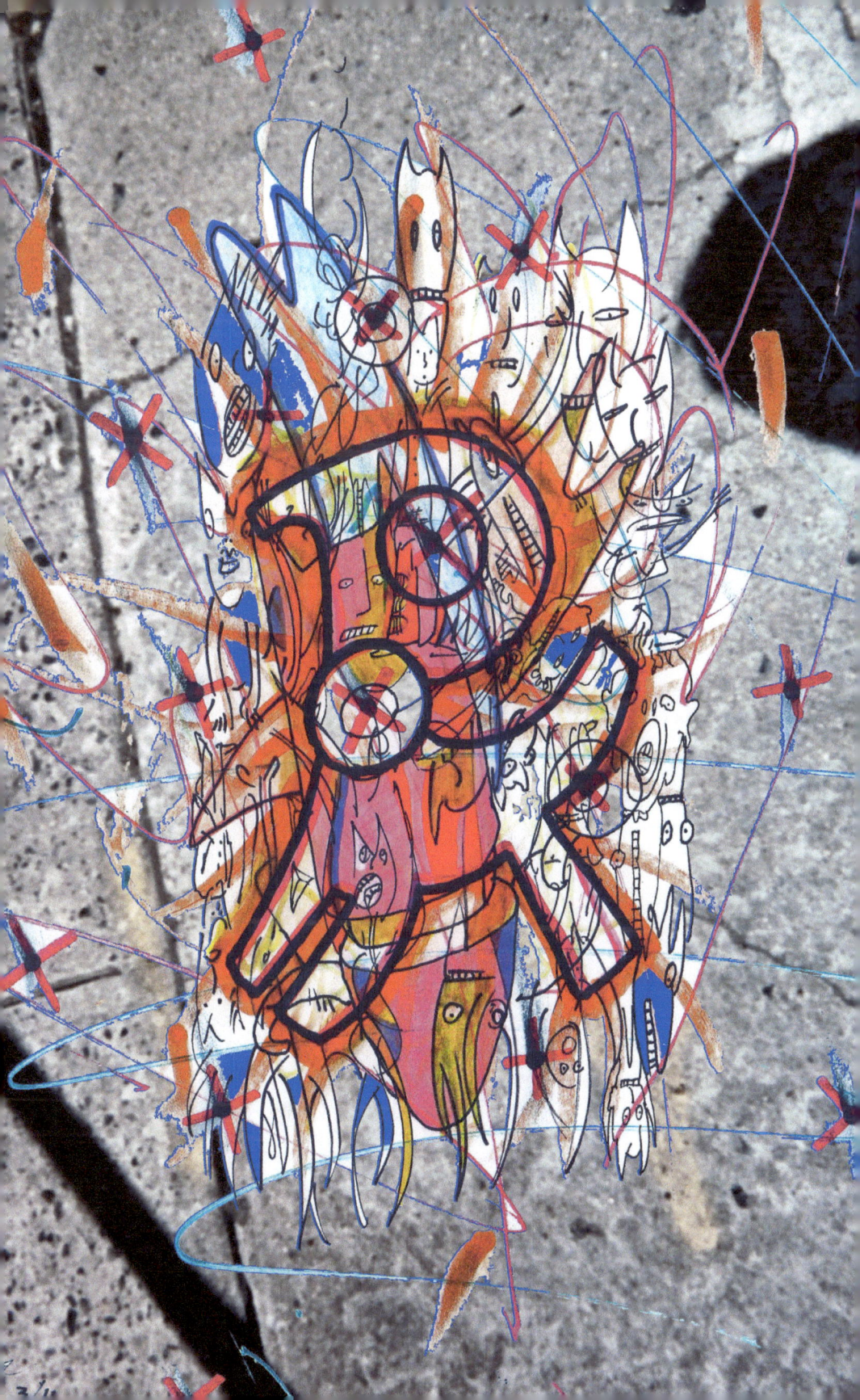

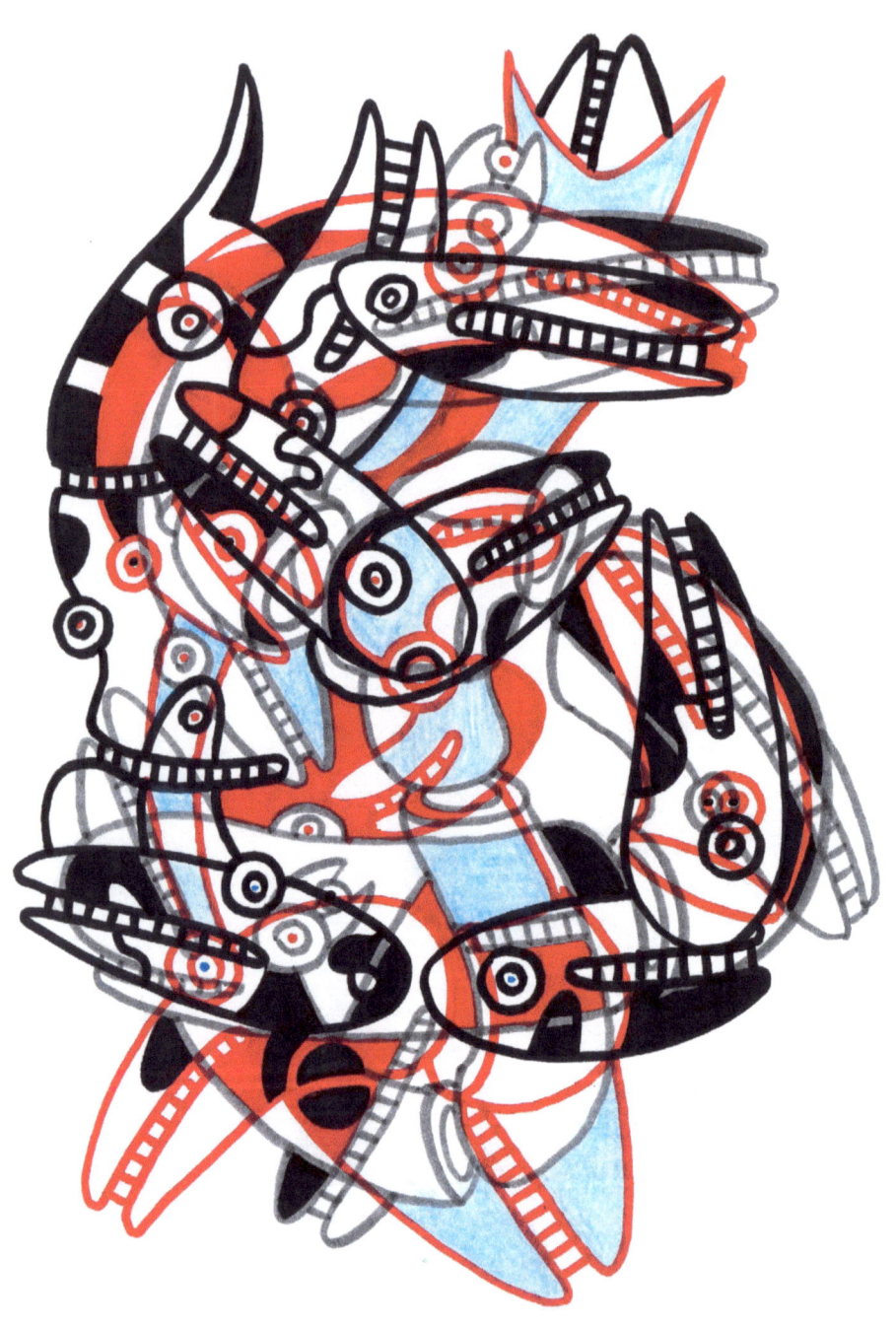

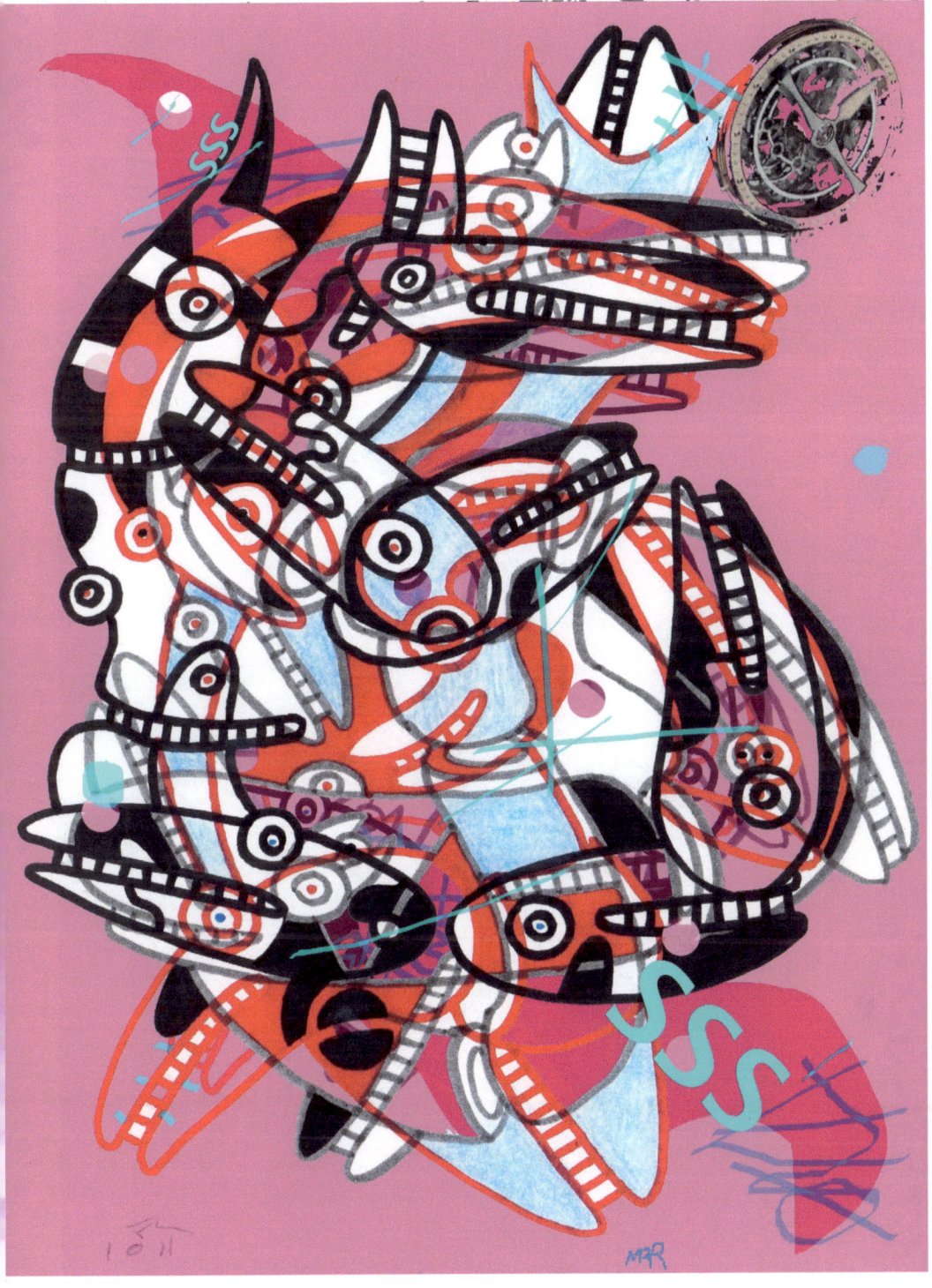

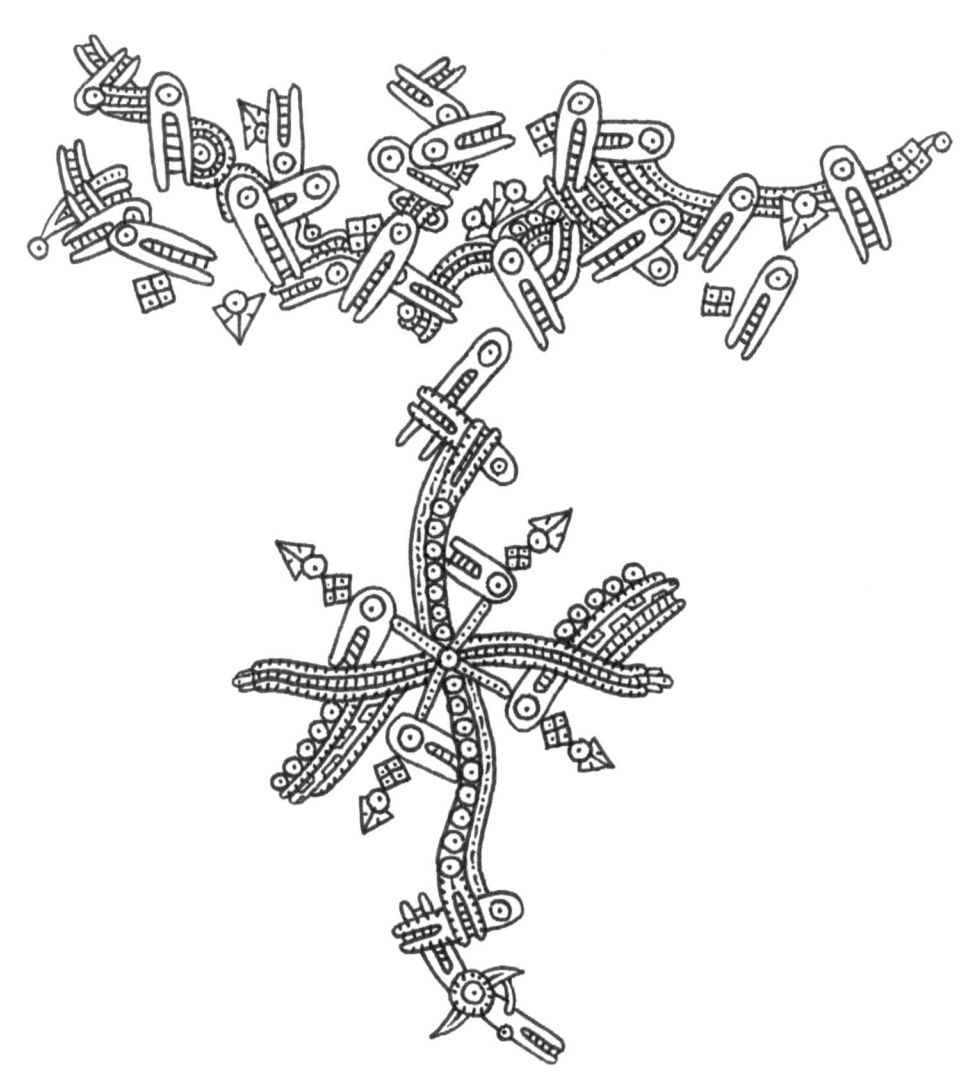

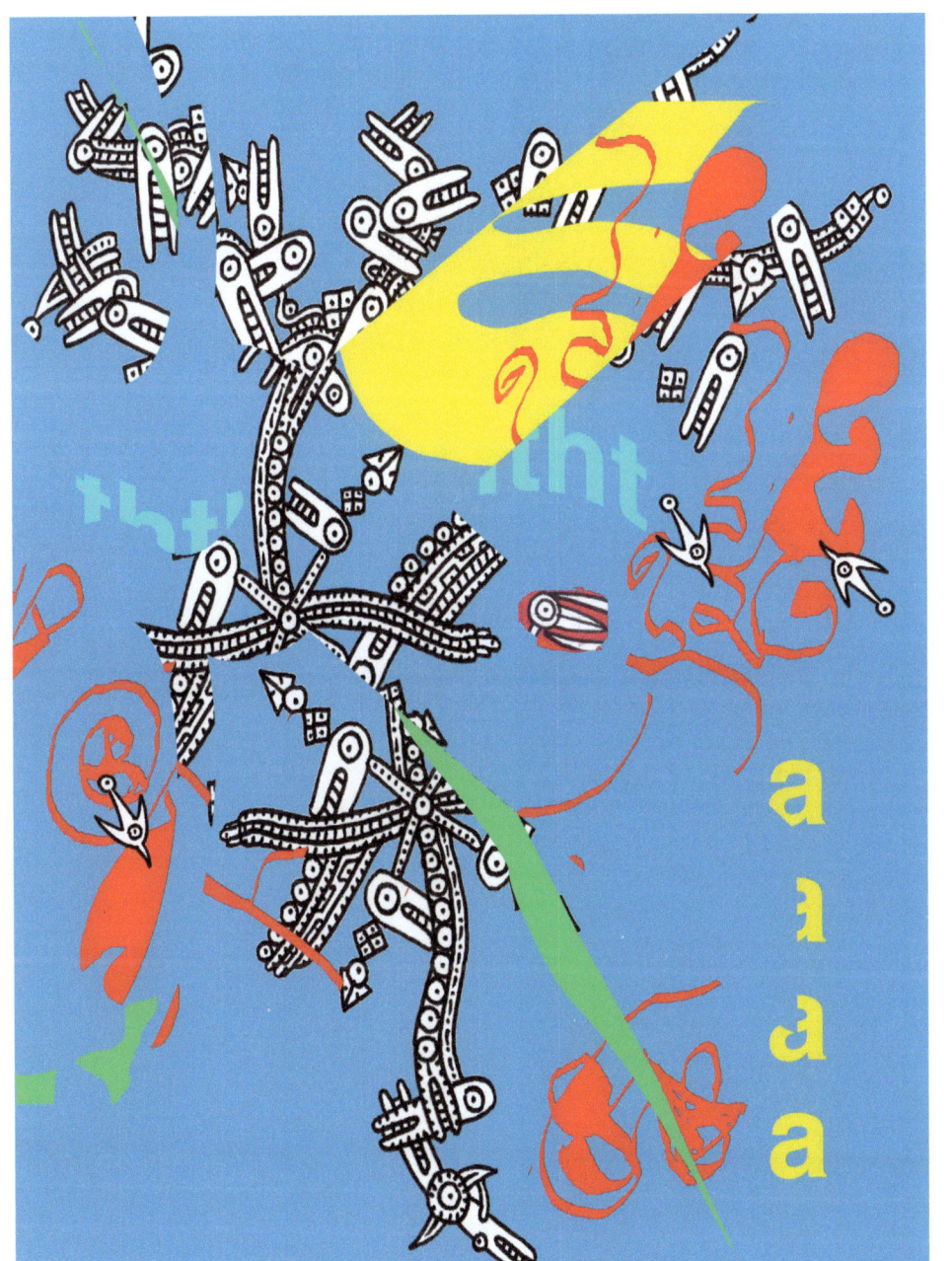

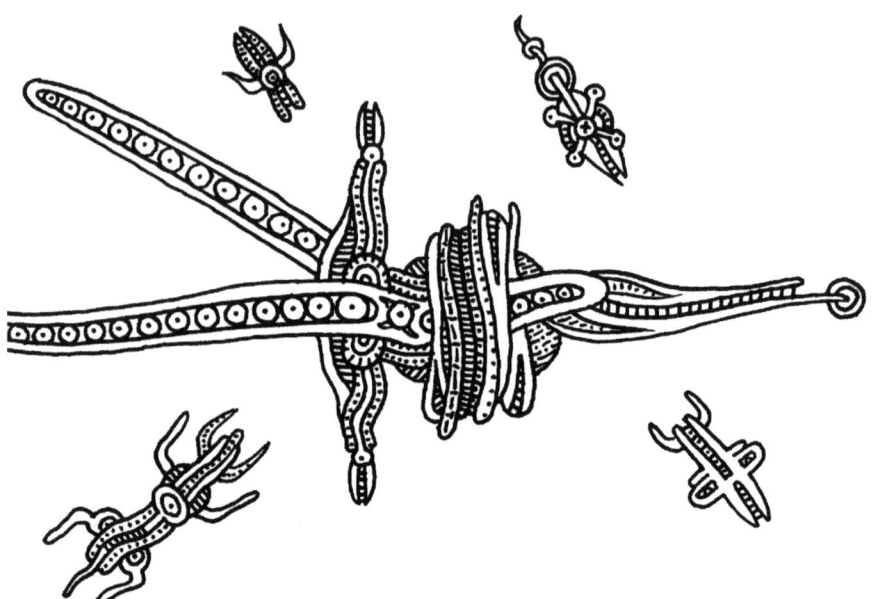

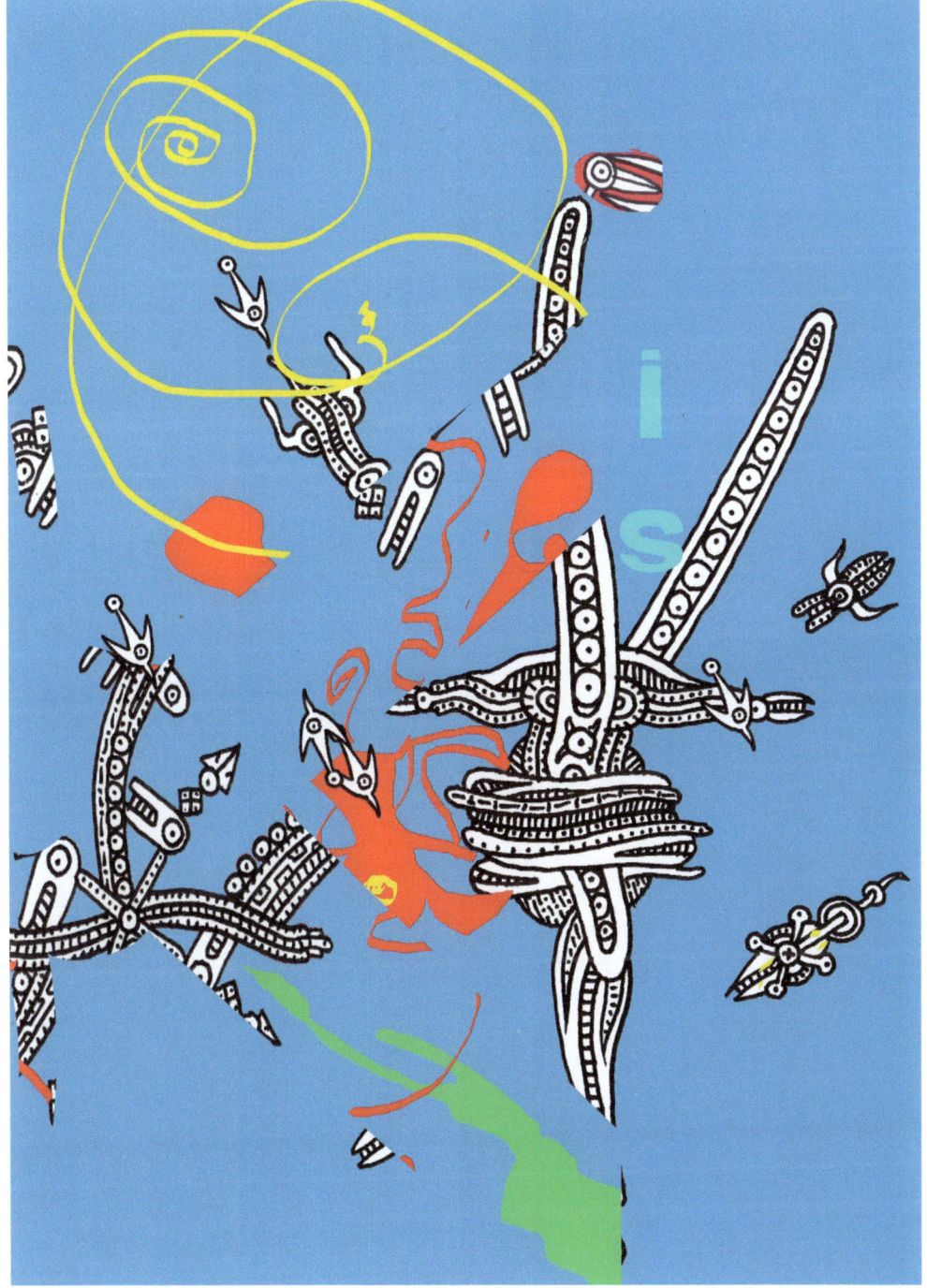

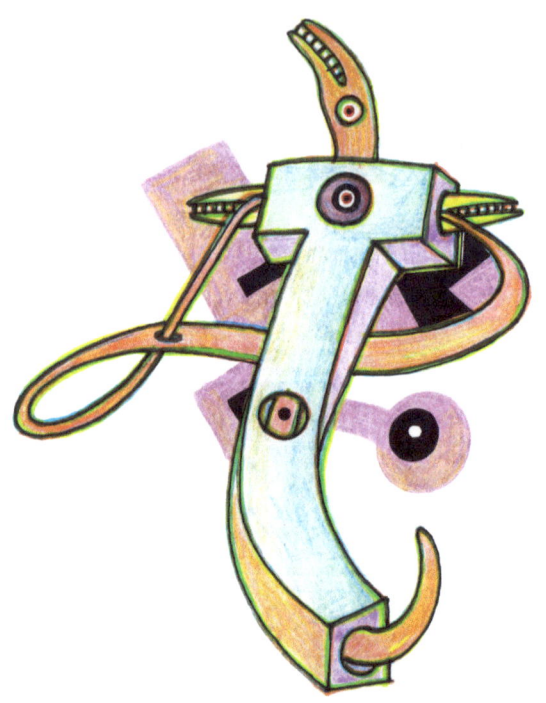

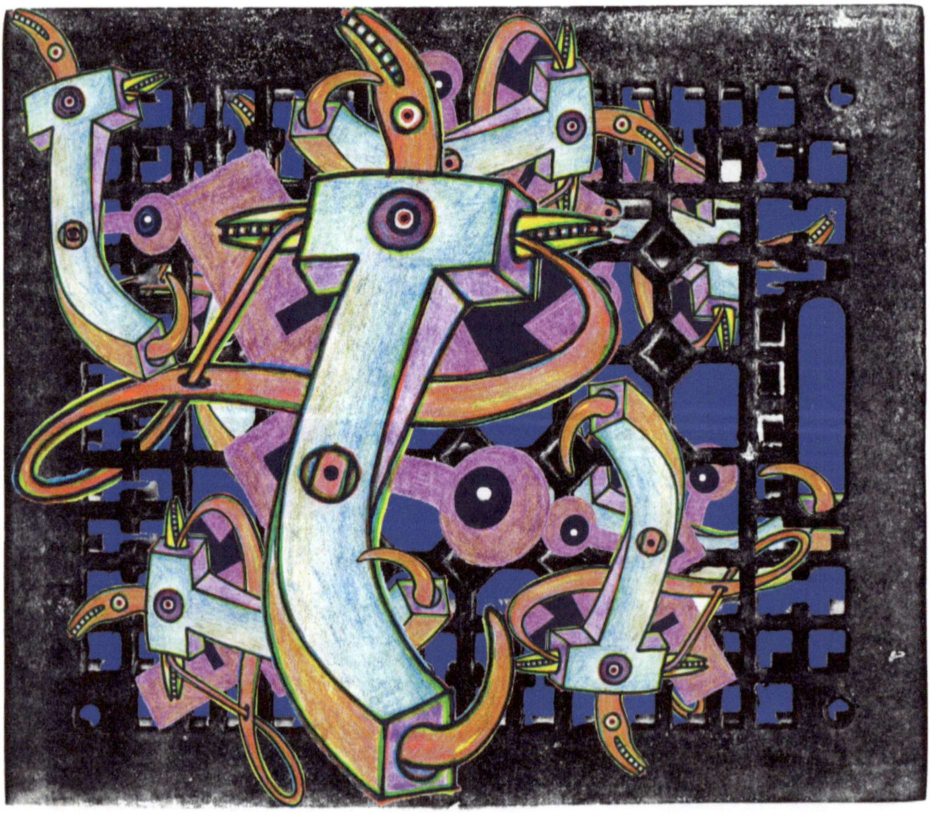

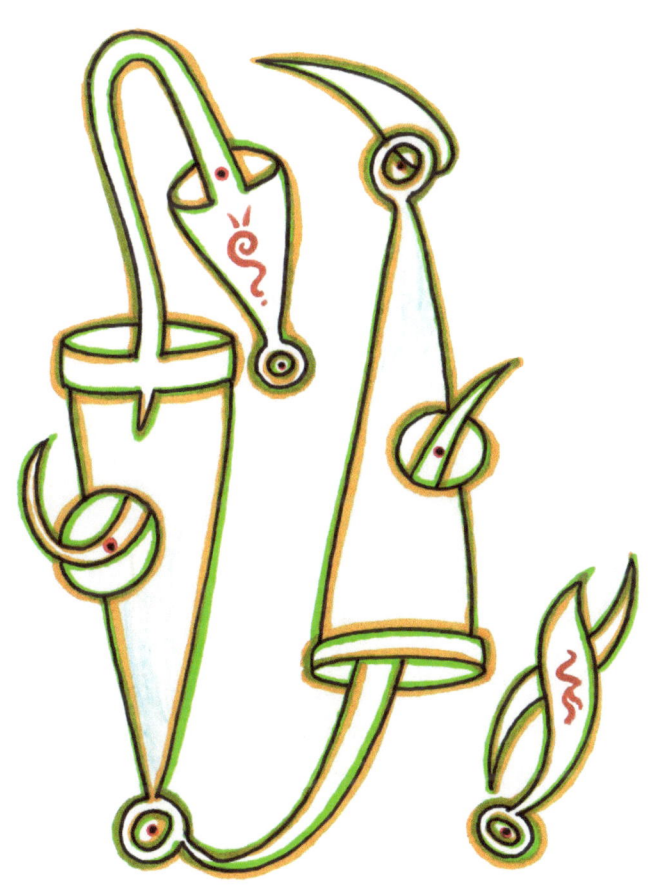

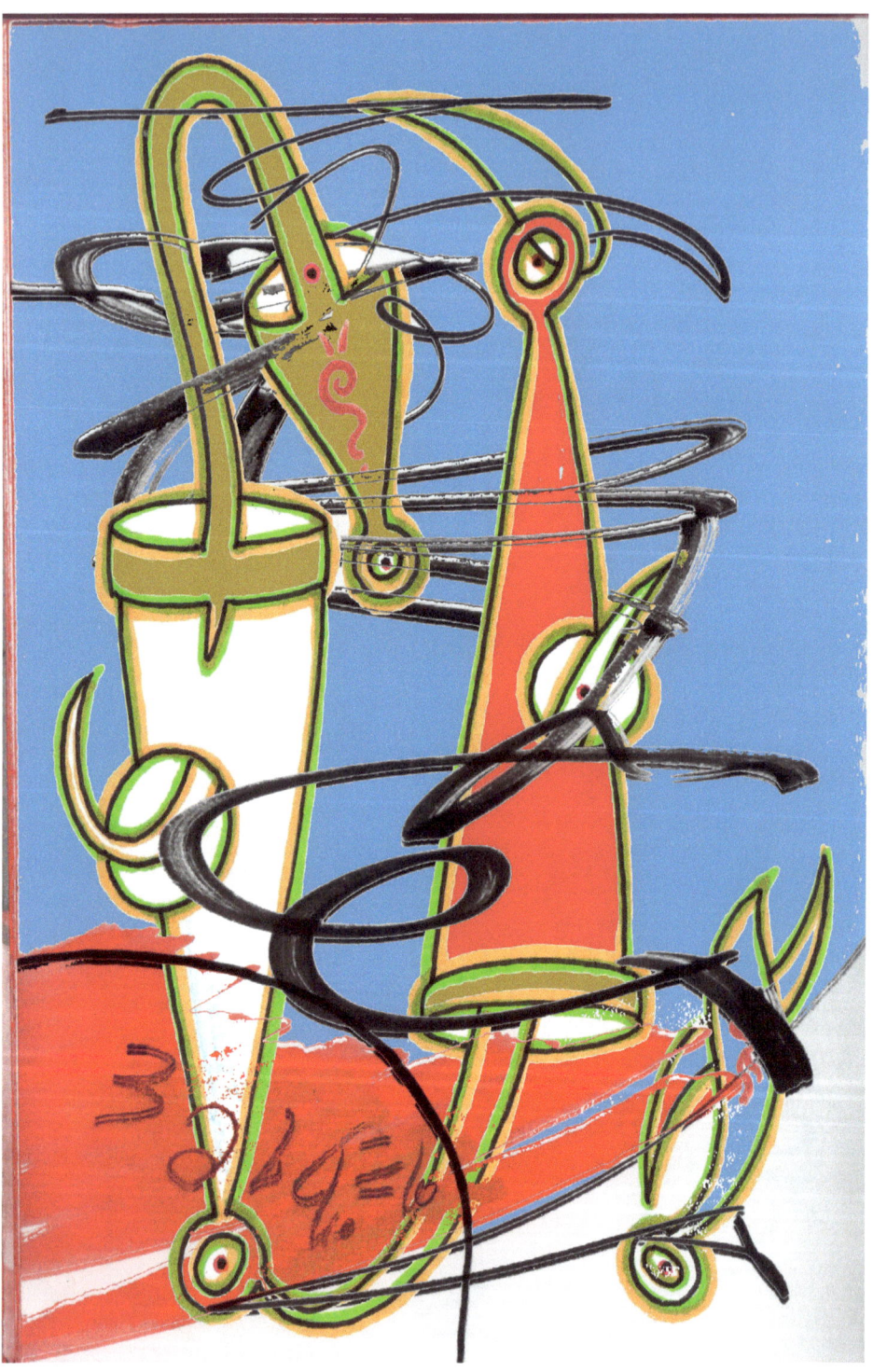

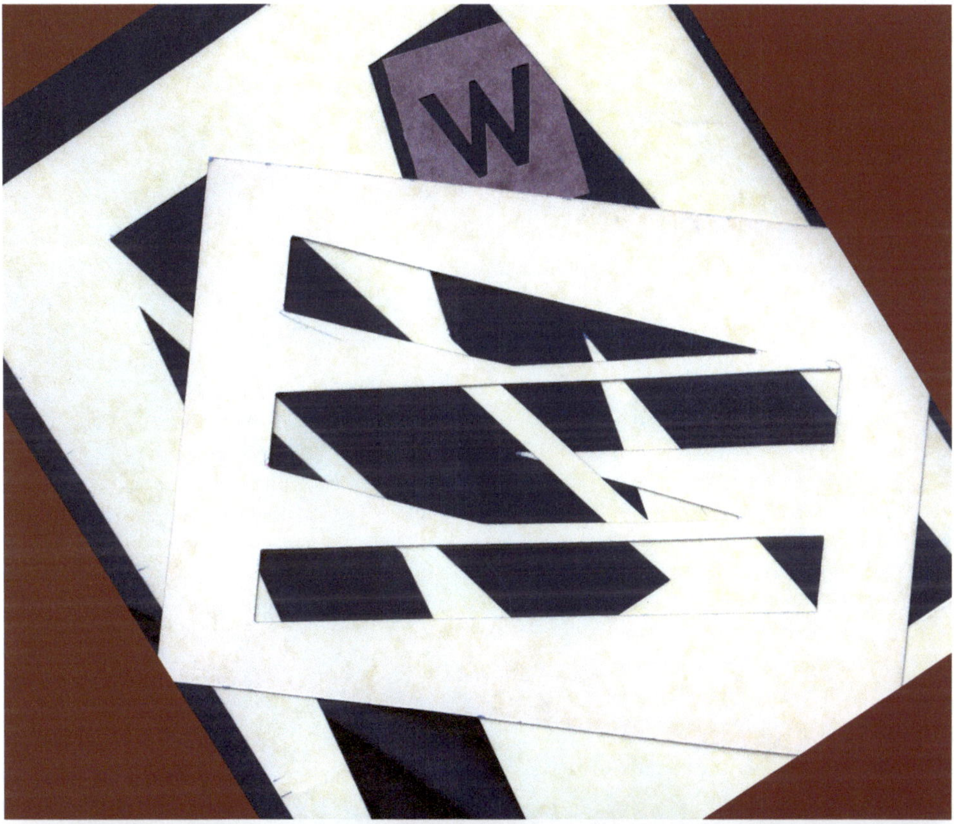

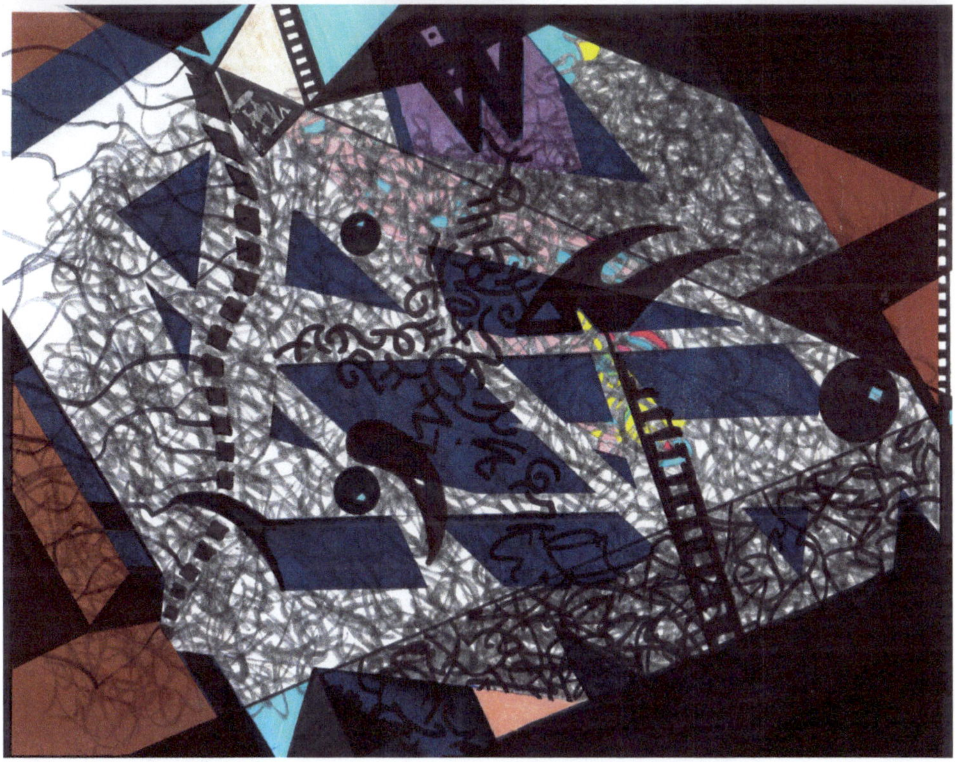

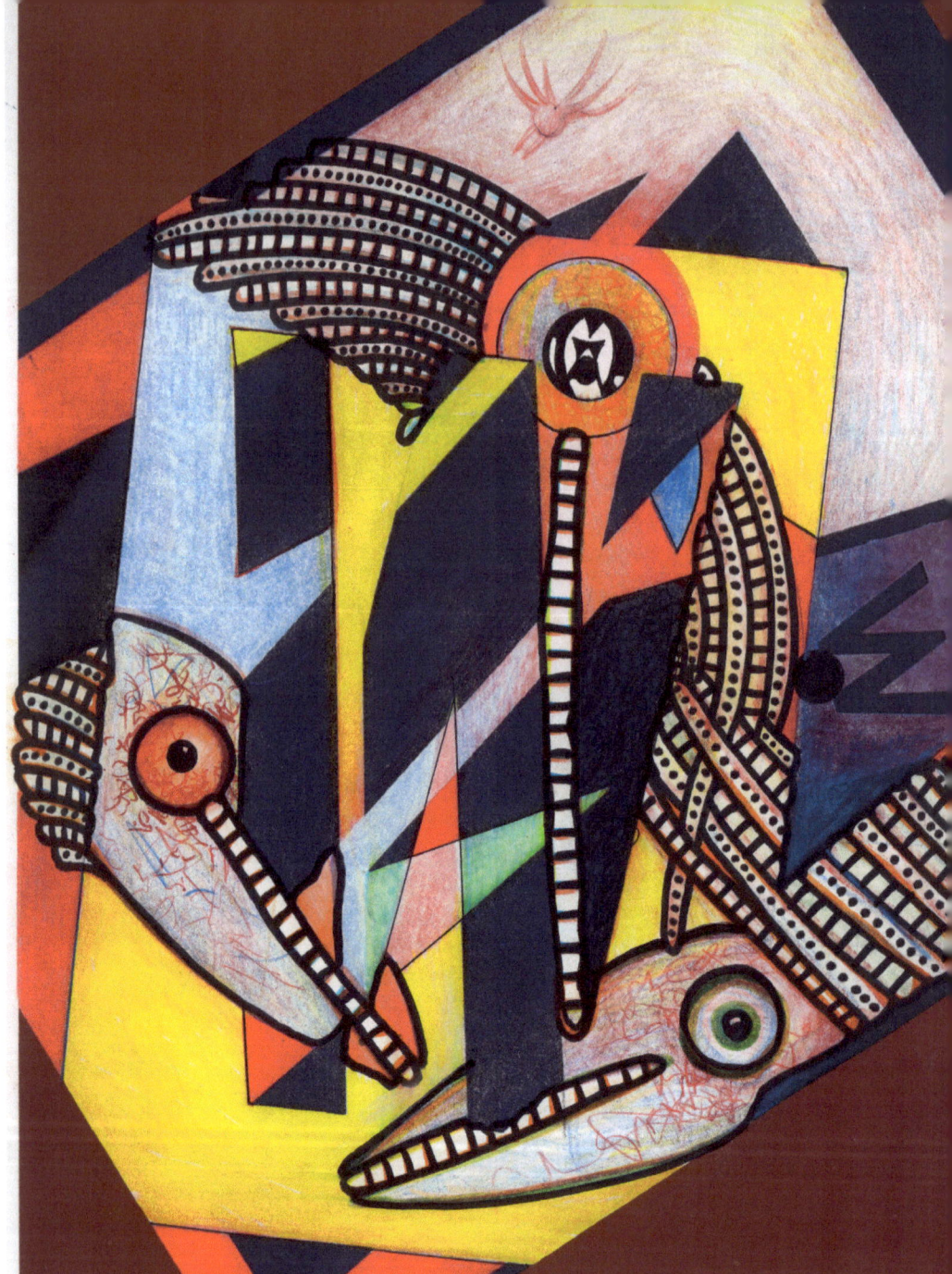

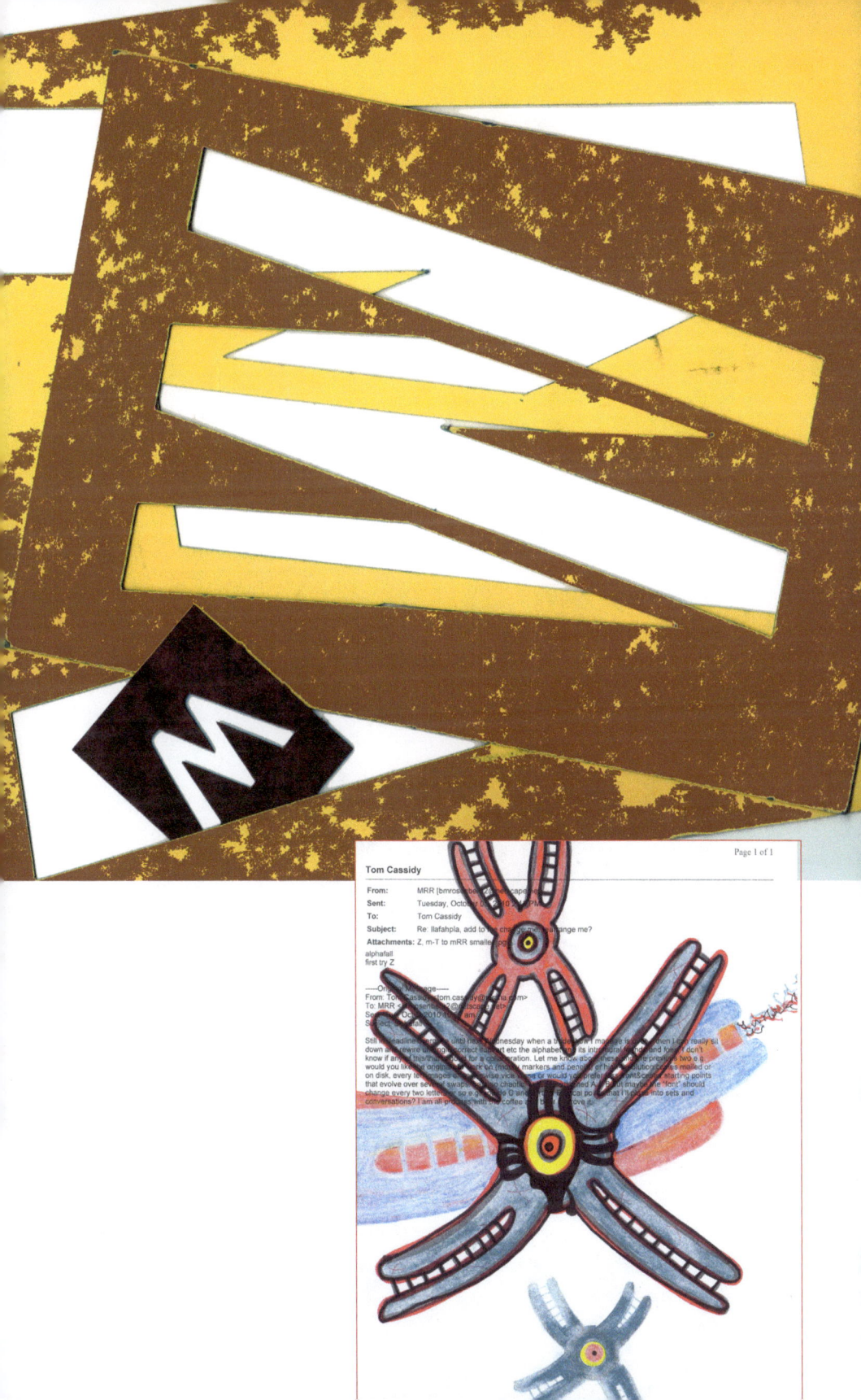

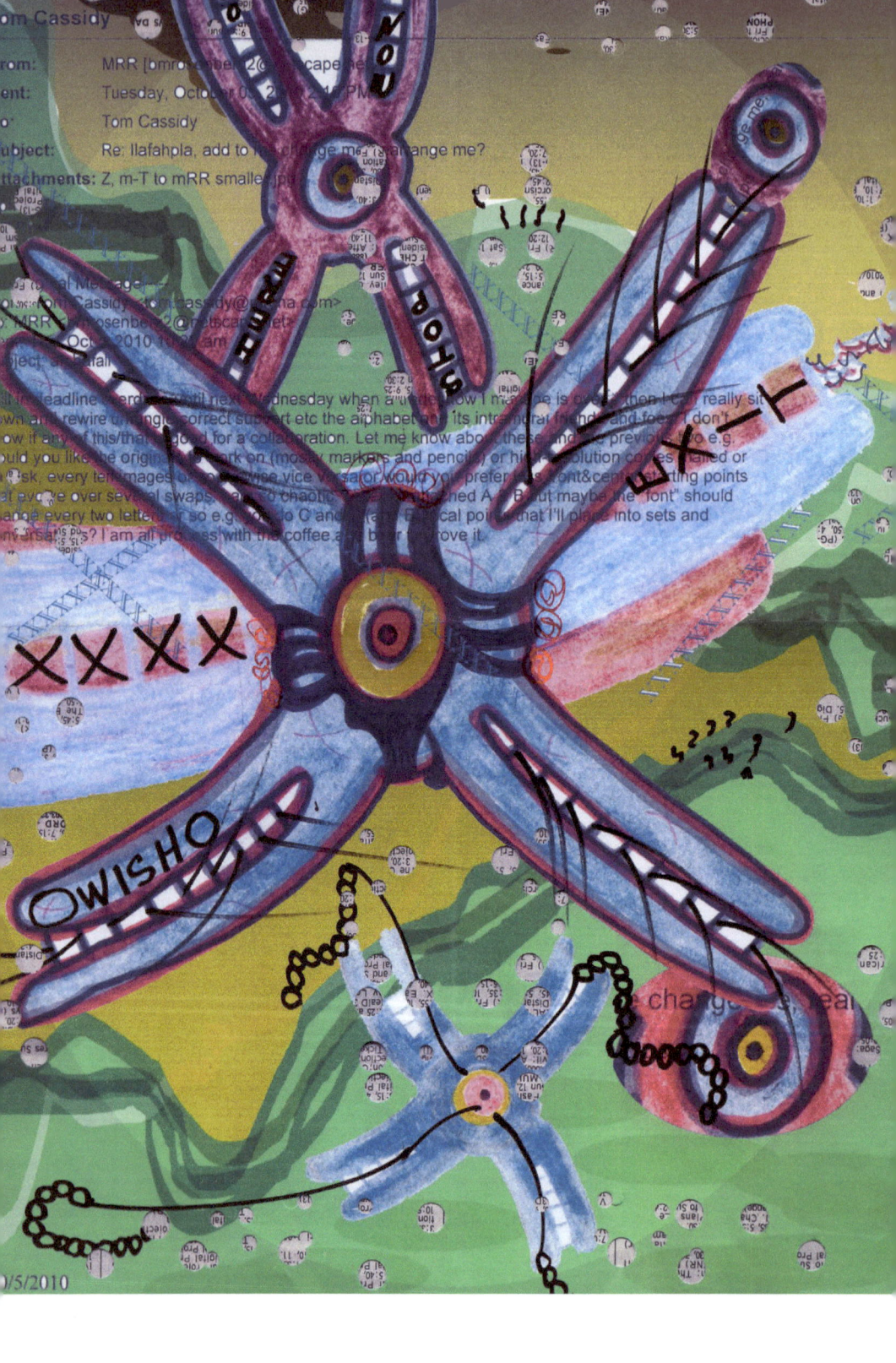

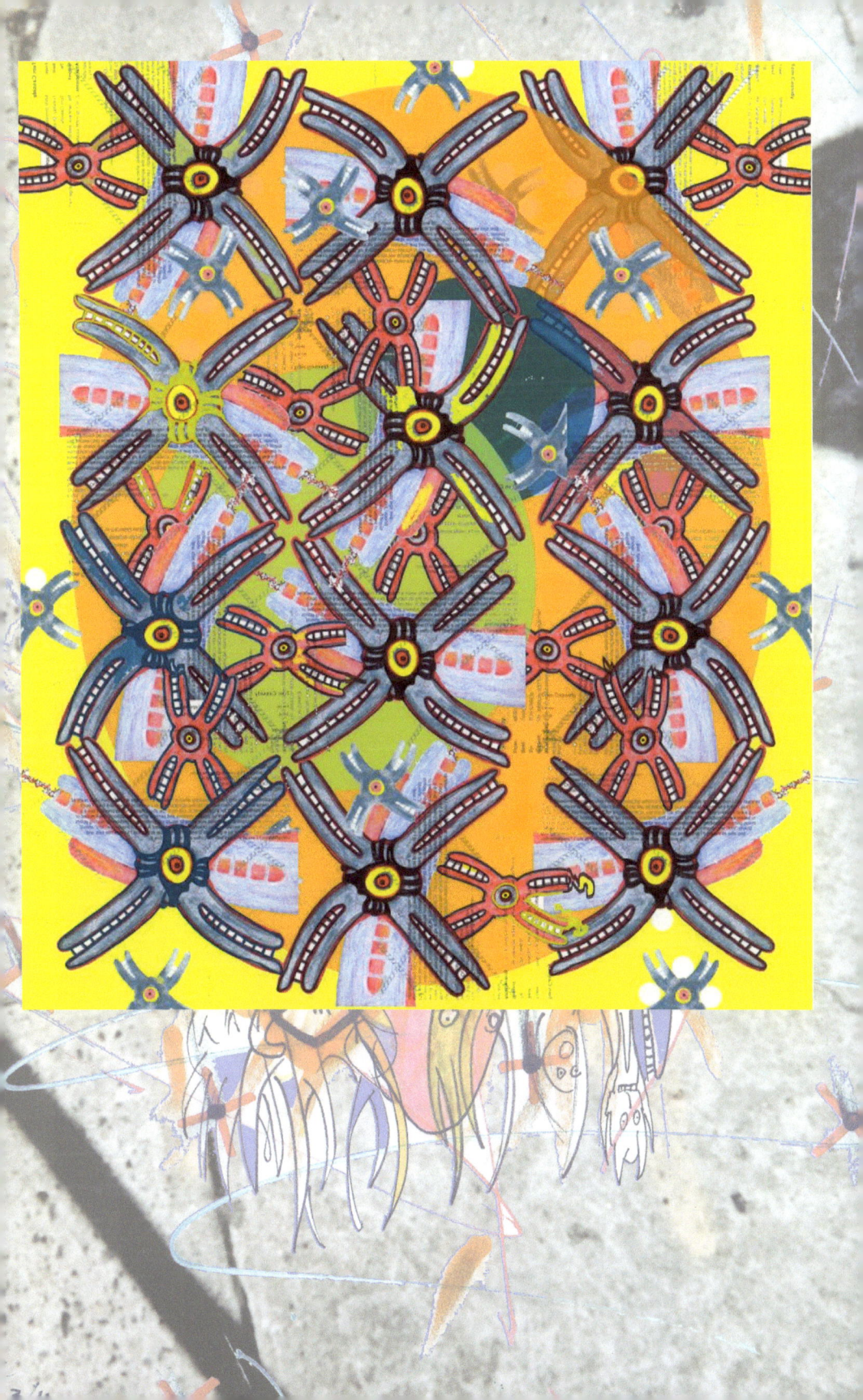

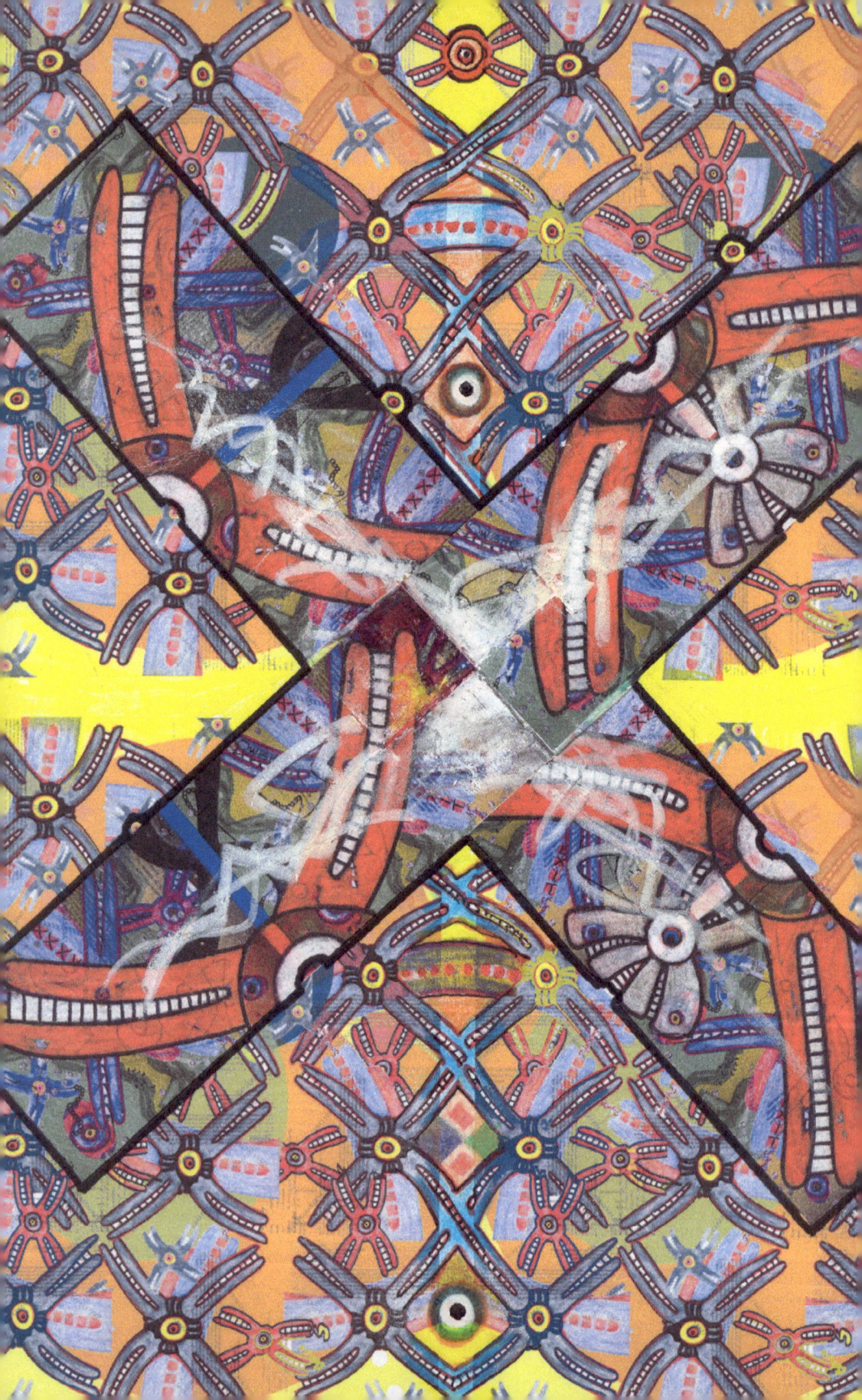

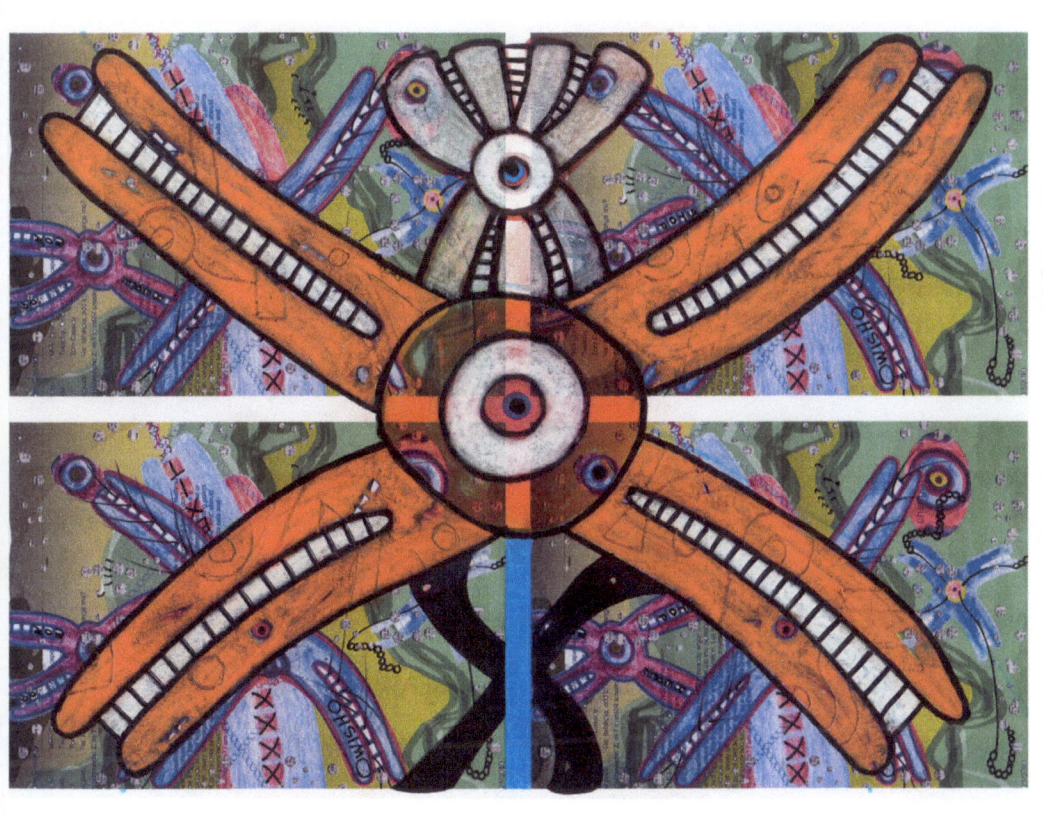

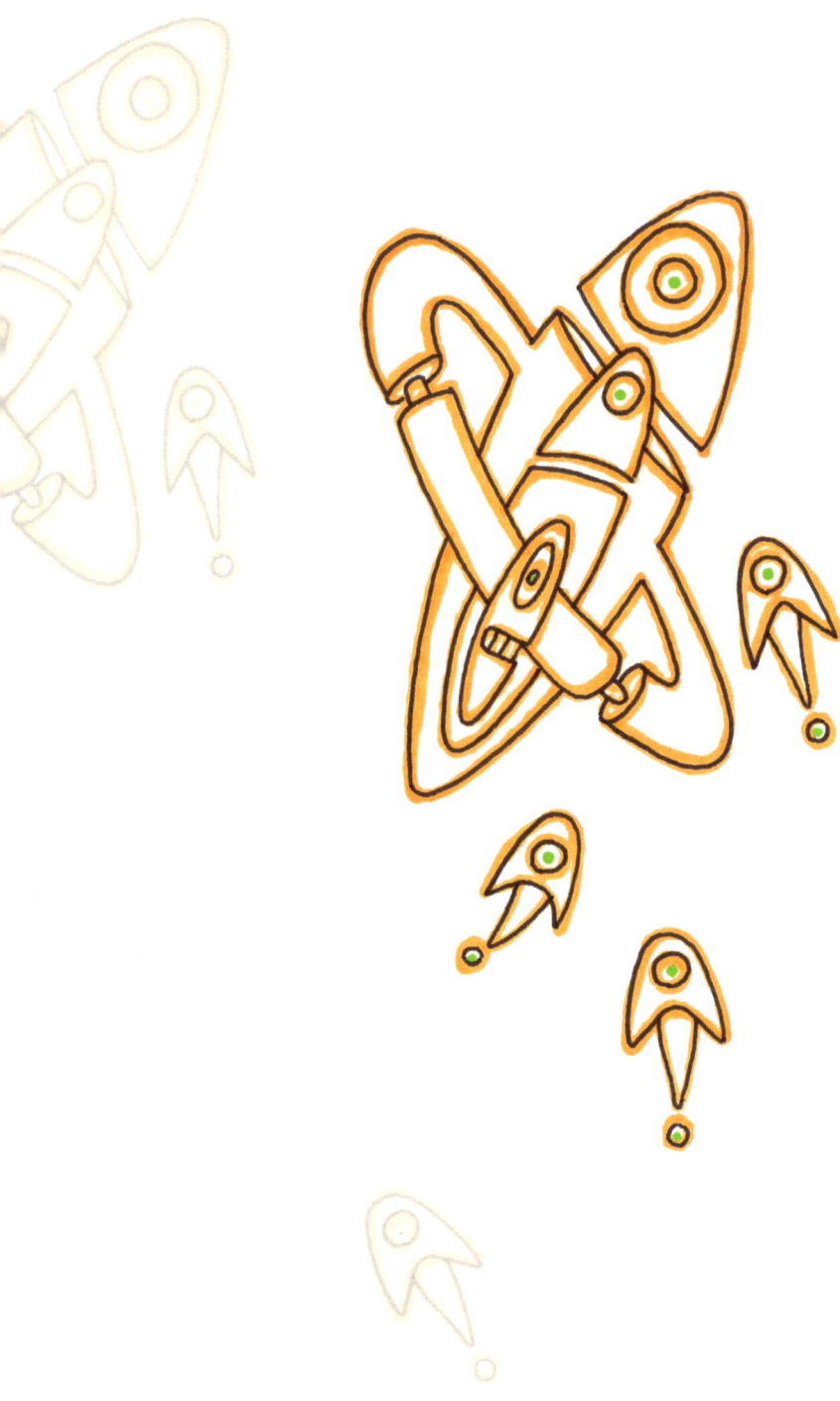

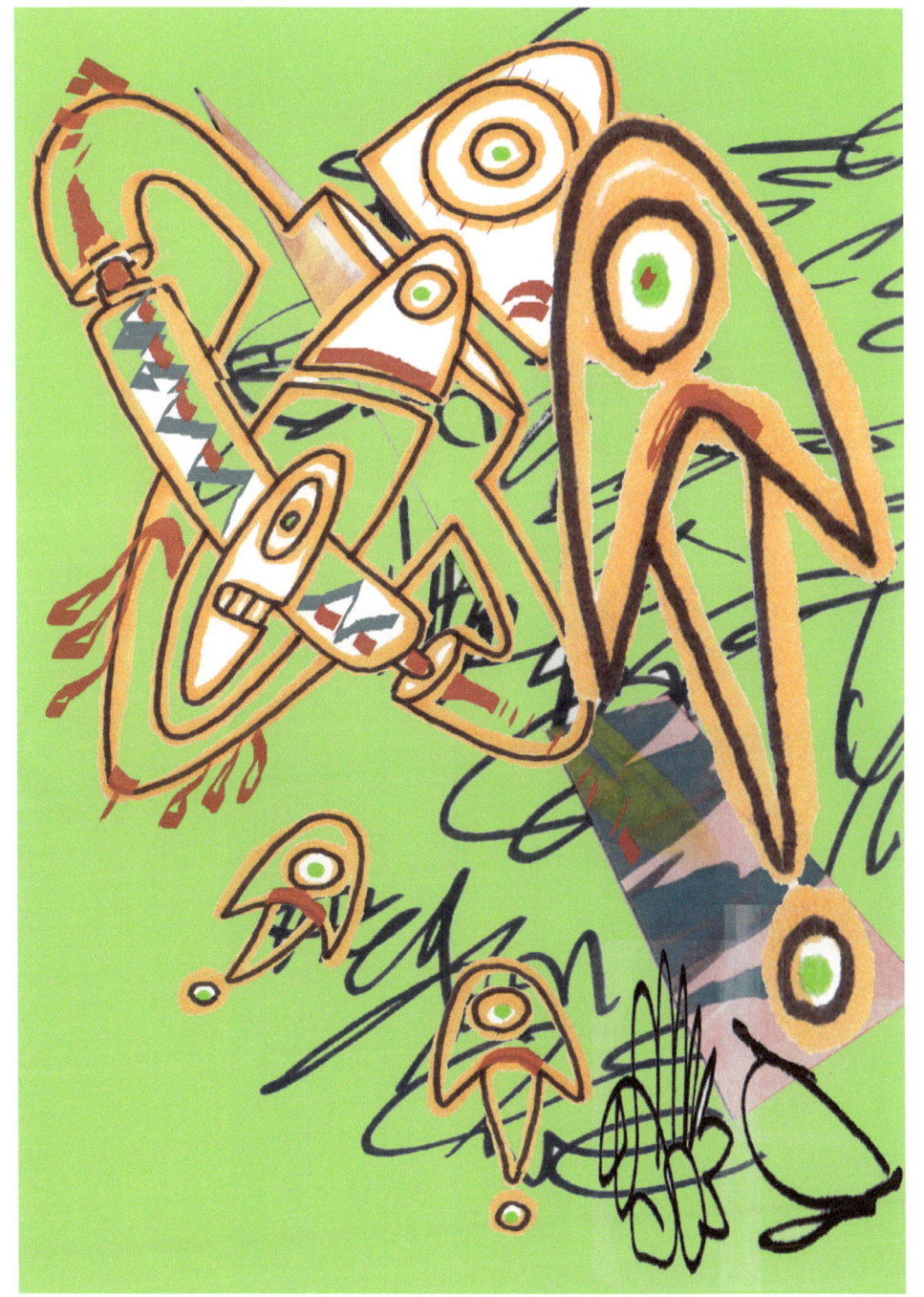

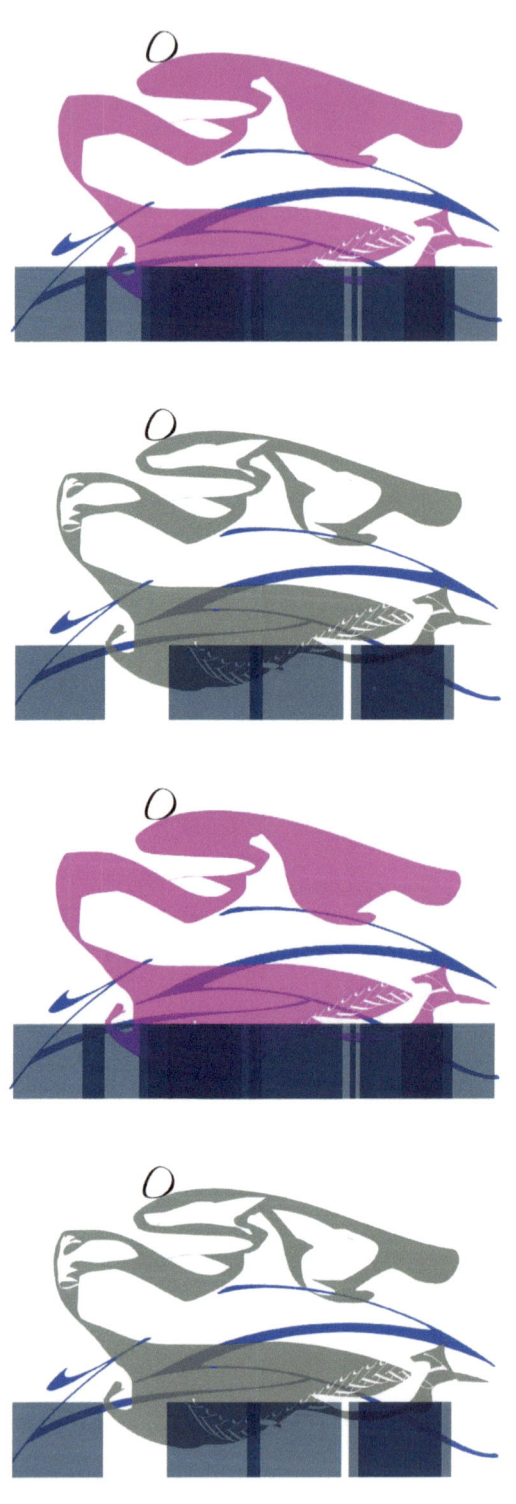

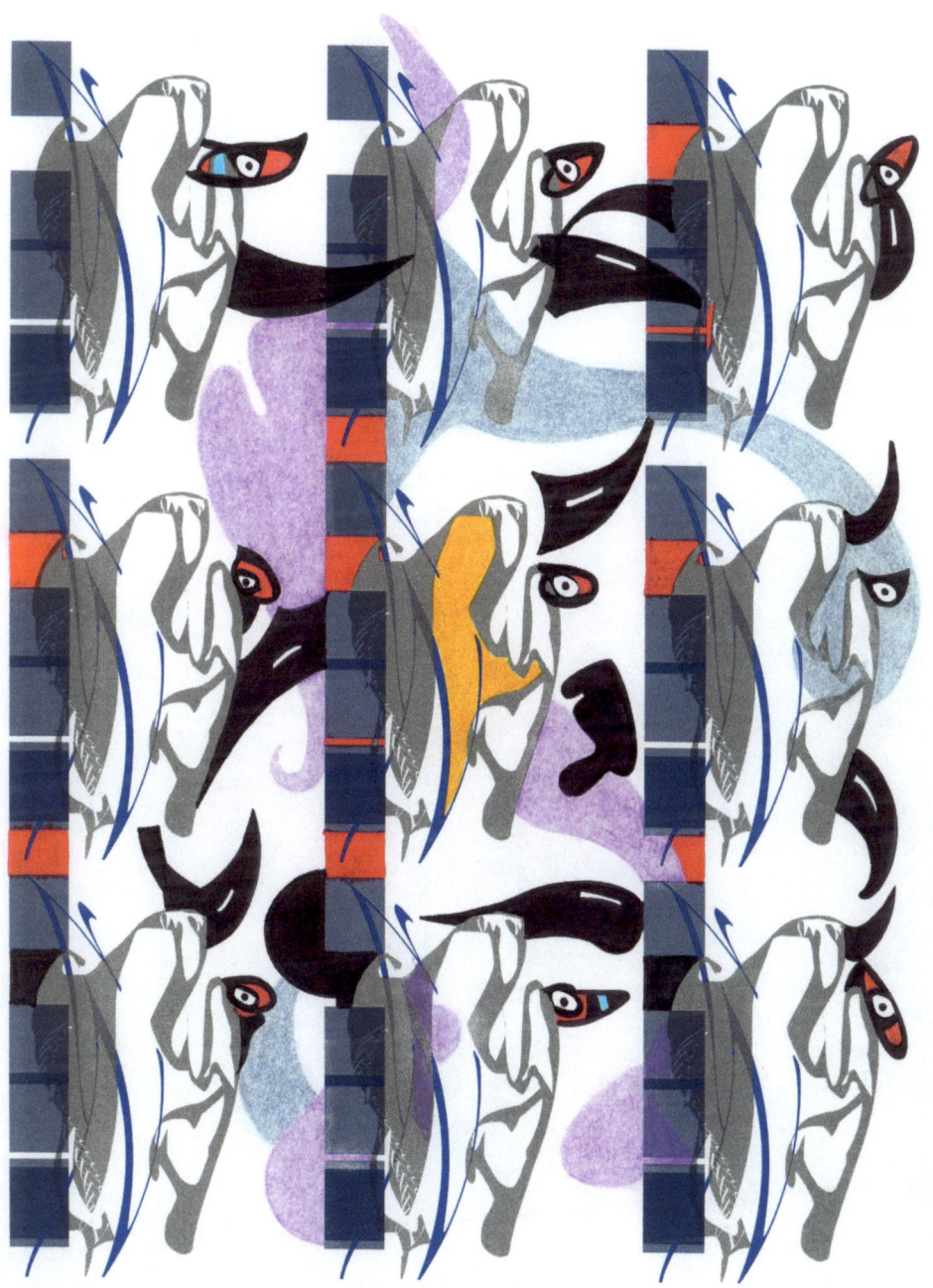

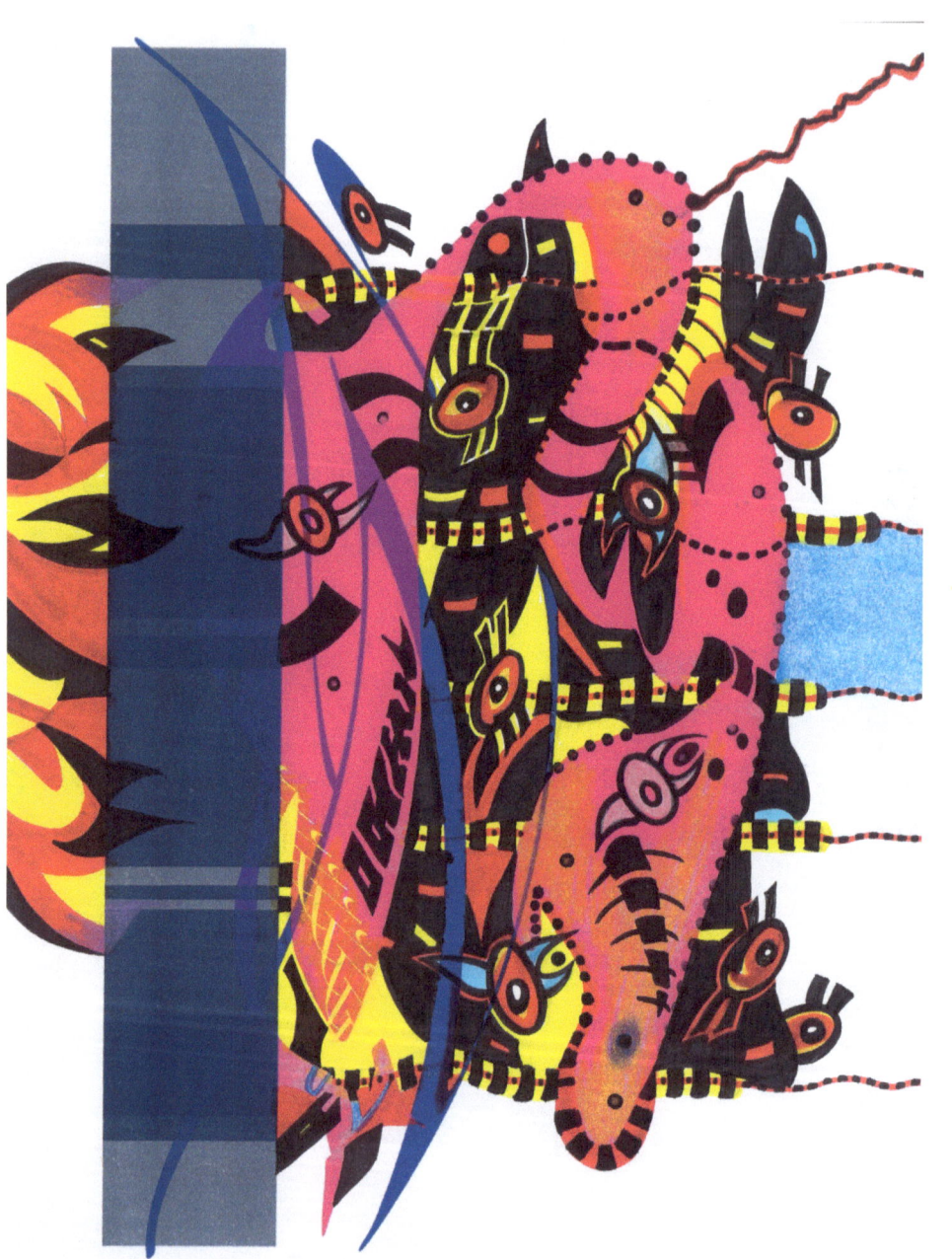

TRIANGLE
(Illus. 17)

Row 1: Ch 2, 1 sc in 2nd ch st from hook, ch 1, turn.
Row 2: 3 sc in sc of Pr R, ch 1, turn.
Row 3: 2 sc in first sc, 1 sc in next sc, 2 sc in last sc, ch 1, turn.
Row 4: 2 sc in first sc, 1 sc in each of next sc, 2 sc in last sc, ch 1.
Continue making as many rows as desired in this manner (inc 1 st at beg and 1 st at end of each row, ch 1 to turn at Beg of each row).

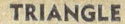
Illus. 17
Triangle

DIAMOND
Begin as for triangle, continue to desired width, then dec 1 st at Beg and 1 st at end of each row (see Dec of sc), ch 1 to turn until 1 st only remains.

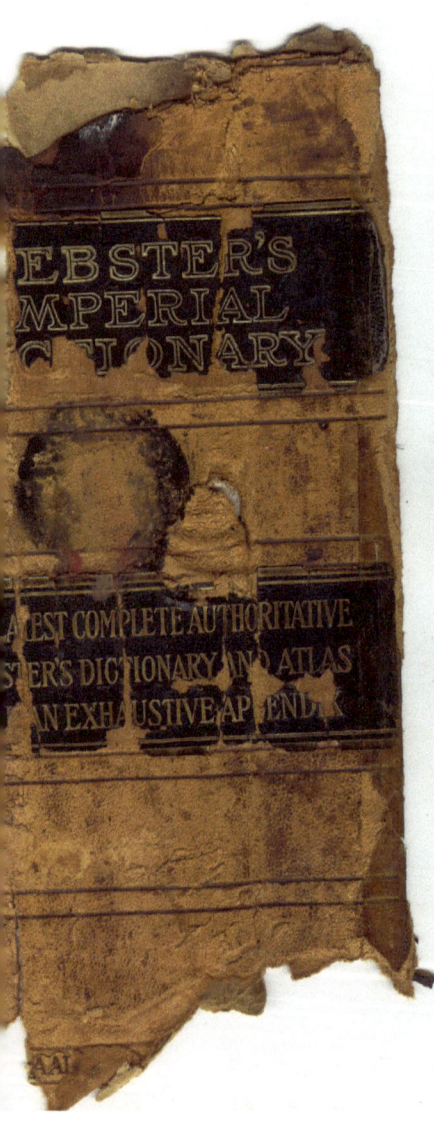

The capital of a is A

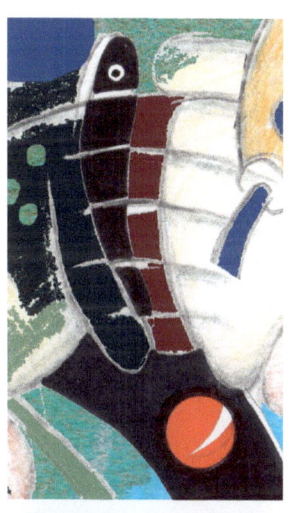
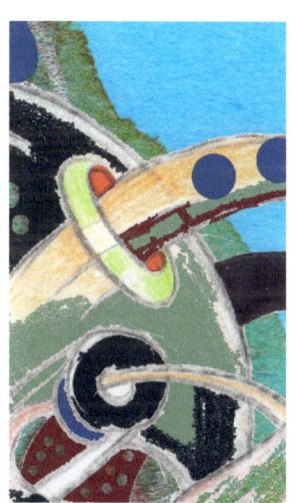
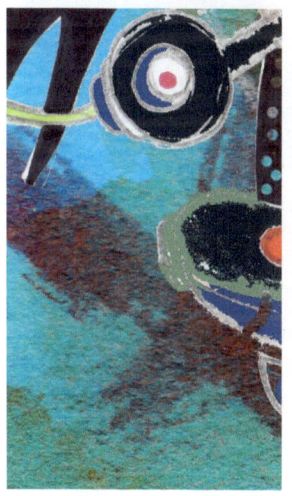
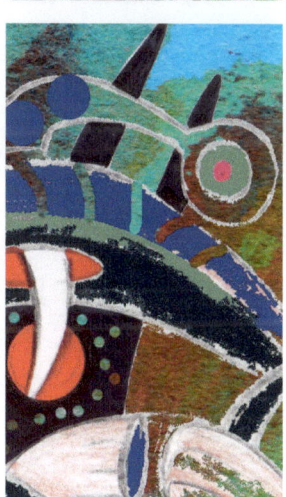

Tom Cassidy's written and drawn works have appeared in hundreds of smallpress and mainstream publications, and in galleries and museums around the world. With John Bennett and Scott Helmes, he co-edited *Vispoeology*, an international anthology of visual literature for the Minnesota Center for Book Arts, where he most recently exhibited 50 Years / 50 Objects from his vast collection of oddities and what-would-without-benefit-of-exhibition-be-called ephemera. Tom (aka Musicmaster) co-founded the Portland performance poetry troupe The Impossibilists, who were reunited in 2008 for a series of shows by the Oregon Heritage Commission. He is a board member and occasional performer with Cheap Theatre and Patrick's Cabaret, often confusing shows with board meetings. All of which sounds far more sane and sober than he'll ever be. His two recent chapbooks (*juiced up walnut* and *give up art*) are commonly avoided.

Marilyn R. Rosenberg's most recent visual poetry in artists' books editions are *NOISE* (2012, Redfoxpress, Ireland); *The Book of Soles (Souls)*, collaboration with C. Mehrl Bennett, (2011, 2013 Luna Bisonte Prods, Columbus OH, USA.); and *RED* (2008, 2013 Otoliths) and also many poems published in various *Otoliths*, Australia. One of a kind bookworks are available at Vamp and Tramp Birmingham AL and Central Booking NYC. MRR's newest visual poem/drawings are at *http://halvard-johnson.blogspot.com/2013/04/marilyn-r-rosenberg.html*; an old one recently appeared on *http://www.thevolta.org/ewc33-mrosenberg-p1.html*. See MRR's older and newer works, with images- *http://scriptjr.nl/issues/2.2/marilyn-r-rosenberg-2-2.php* and *http://local-artists.org/users/marilyn-r-rosenberg*. Images of works are in print publications: *LAST VISPO ANTHOLOGY: Visual Poetry 1998 - 2008*; *1000 ARTISTS' BOOKS; EXPLORING THE BOOK AS ART*; and *WOMEN IN THE ARTI-STAMP SPOTLIGHT*. Also, MRR is expecting a group of surprises.

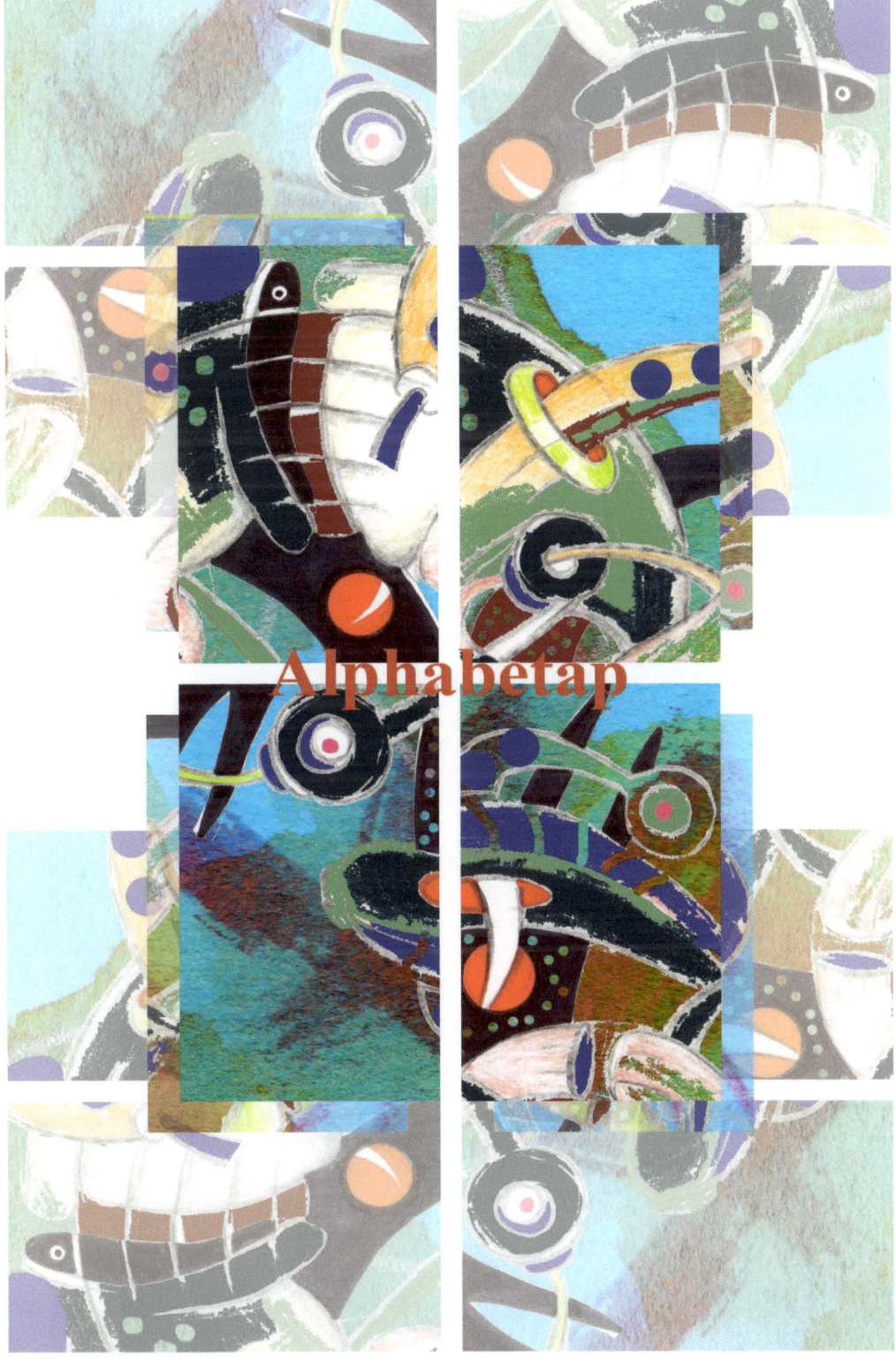

www.ingramcontent.com/pod-product-compliance
Lightning Source LLC
Chambersburg PA
CBHW040226220526
45473CB00001B/133